"A well-worn copy of this playbook should be in every sales leader's briefcase. As a leader, I understand and value the lessons Nathan shares in this book not as theory, but as proven practices."

Rick Kimsey
CEO
Advanced Wireless

"The *Sales Leaders Playbook* is for any sales leader looking to increase their sales. This book teaches proven skills and lessons that will deliver sustainable results year after year after year. 'Be Progressive' and make this rocking book part of your business plan!"

Dean Lindsay
Author of The Progress Principle and
Cracking the Networking CODE

"As a sales leader that has driven many people and many personalities to success historically, the playbook really is a winner! The book will open your eyes and really inspire action. All leaders find themselves in struggling situations; this book really helps dissect those and helps you take action! You will NOT want to put this book down!"

Derek Bailey
Executive Sales Area Director
Sprint

"This book is the ultimate playbook for any sales organization competing in today's business world."

Ivan Misner
NY Times Bestselling Author and
Founder of BNI

"This book is written from personal failures and successes. The adage 'been there, done that' aptly describes Nathan as one of the few superior sales executives who was able to parlay that success to develop into an outstanding sales leader and motivator."

Brad Mitchel
Executive Vice President of International Accounts
Cable and Wireless

"There are a lot of sales books on the market that focus too much on the psychology of selling-and not on the blocking and tackling that's necessary to build winning teams and execute consistently-that is what this book delivers and more."

Scott C. Whitaker
President and CEO
Whitaker & Company

"Nathan offers great insight and provides a common sense approach to sales management. In my 19 years of outside sales experience I have read numerous books devoted to increasing sales efficiencies. Nathan's ideas shed new light on common challenges in the quest for sales improvement."

Rick Epstein
Austin Toros
NBA D-League Vice President of Sales

"These practices have made a difference in my success as a sales leader."

Brian Olsen
Director of National Accounts
Extended Stay Hotels

"Winning is what the game is all about. Quality coaching is the key to winning. *The Sales Leaders Playbook* shows you and your team how to be winners!"

Ben Lange
President
America's Auto Auction

"… *The Sales Leaders Playbook*" is refreshing, a simple but important message, that encompasses a lot of personal best practices that I have found to be essential keys to success and building quality teams."

Ray Barnes
Vice President – Sales
Extended Stay Hotels

"*The Sales Leaders Playbook* is a great read. It brings back to mind many of the techniques and methods that we lose focus of throughout the day to day grind. I would highly recommend this book to anyone in the business world."

Kevin Ayres
CEO
Pump It Up

THE SALES LEADERS
PLAYBOOK

Nathan Jamail

SCOOTER PUBLISHING, INC.

SCOOTER PUBLISHING, INC.°

Scooter Publishing
2591 Dallas Parkway
Suite 300
Frisco, TX 75034

Library of Congress Control Number – 2008904266
ISBN – 978-0-9817789-0-7

2nd Edition

Printed in the United States

DEDICATION

I dedicate this book to all of my fellow
sales people and sales leaders. May this information
help you achieve the same success as it has for me.

ACKNOWLEDGMENTS

When you see a Grammy winner or any other famous person accepting an award get up to give an acceptance speech, a small groan from inside probably rattles around within you. The important truth though is that this person has some true heartfelt thanks for persons that without their help that famous person would not be standing there boring you to tears.

Well, start groaning, or flip the page, as I have many people who have contributed to not only the publication of this book, but also to whom I have become today.

As I say in my seminars and workshops, 90% of the information I share with my clients or share with you in this book I learned from someone else. I have found in my experience that most people I have had the opportunity to work with were much smarter than I, more experienced than I, yet I had the desire and ability to learn from them.

I want to first thank my wife, who is my best friend and business partner. Without her I would still be trying to figure out how to complete the first chapter. Shannon is one of the most amazing people I have ever met in my life, and I am lucky to call her my wife.

I also would like to thank many of the leaders I have had over the past eighteen years. I have been very fortunate to have worked with and learned from great mentors. The lessons they have taught me have enabled much of my corporate and entrepreneur success. Thanks to Mark Hood who took a chance and hired a nineteen-year-old kid to sell life and health insurance. Thanks to Gary Sullivan who took the time to help me create my first real business plan and had the tough conversation with me about what I needed to do to get to the next level. Thanks to Brad Mitchell, who gave me my first management job at twenty-four years of age. He taught me to become responsible for a team and held me accountable to the highest standards. Thanks to Jim Moreland, mentor and friend, who showed me how a team would unconditionally follow a leader. And thanks to all of the other great leaders I have had the opportunity to work with in my career and life.

I would like to thank my parents for everything they have done for me over my lifetime. To my mother, who is my friend and keeps me on the right path, I sincerely thank you. And to my father, who is also my business partner and mentor, offering sound advice and help even when I am not smart enough to ask for it, I offer you my heartfelt thanks and gratitude.

Each of the above mentioned, and more, taught me something I still use in my business today along with many of the ideas I share with you in this book. To the hundreds of team members and peers I have had over the past ten years, thank you for the roads traveled both smooth and rough.

I would like to thank The Trade Group for creating an awesome book cover.

I would like to thank Joe Calloway, whom I called shortly after I got in the speaking and writing business. He not only offered to help, but believed in me enough to support me.

Lastly, I would like to thank the many friends and family members that have encouraged and believed in me.

CONTENTS

INTRODUCTION

I remember one Sunday afternoon when my brain started to wander while watching the Dallas Cowboys play the Minnesota Vikings. Instead of arm-chair quarter backing the game, I began thinking about how in the business world we use a lot of sports analogies.

This of course makes sense because there are tons of similarities between a successful football team and a successful sales team. They both must have a great leader, draft the best players every year, practice regularly, focus on the basic fundamentals of blocking and tackling, execute, minimize turn-overs in employees (good ones at least), and lose deals to the competition. They both rely on teamwork, positive mental attitudes, strong belief systems, motivated team members, and so on.

The correlation between sports and business led me to pursue this concept further. After exploring the concept with my business mentors and peers, I ultimately decided to write this book.

I am not a writer by trade. I am, however, a seasoned sales leader, and it is from this experience that I write this book. For fifteen years, I carried a sales bag and led sales teams across the United States. During my tenure, I learned and grew through my experiences in the board room and the streets. I was taught by the greatest school (and I am not referring to the colleges I attended). I was taught by the school of *hard work*. Some of the greatest professional lessons I learned came from my leaders, peers, employees and customers.

Over the years, I have experienced great success along with failure. Both types of experiences have strengthened me and made me into a better person. But here is how I look at it: as long as I keep trying, I am always moving forward.

I have implemented my playbook for success several hundred times with individuals and teams. Without fail, those who desired success and believed they could be successful – *achieved success.* It is a phrase that is used too often so that it has become dull and mainstream. But the truth of this entire book (and your success) is: "If you believe you can do it, you will."

ARE THERE NATURAL BORN SALESPEOPLE?

In my professional lifetime I have heard many sales people and sales leaders express their desire to be "as good as someone else, who is a natural born sales person (*or* natural born leader)." In response, I always asked them, "So, what is stopping you?" And from my experience, the only one acceptable answer to this question is, "Me." *Each one of us* is the one that controls our talents, abilities, and (most importantly) success.

But the real truth is that no one is born great at anything. People may have inherent talents, but they must practice to be great at a set skill. Take Tiger Woods, who is not a natural born golfer. Sure he may have been born with talent, but he had to *practice* and *learn* how to be the "best golfer in history."

It is a common misconception that someone is born great. All too often, this belief is used as an *excuse* for those who are not succeeding rather than a *compliment* to the ones who are dedicated and willing to practice to be great. It is much easier to say "Joe is a natural born leader" than "I do not want to work as hard as Joe." Now, I am not saying that some people are not trying to be complimentary in the phrase, but more often than not folks are just using the "natural born" phrase as a self-imposed limitation and excuse.

In the game of basketball, one could easily say that someone can be too short to play. If that is completely true, then what about Spud Webb? He was only 5 feet, 7 inches tall. He played 12 seasons in the NBA and won the slam dunk contest in 1986.

What about Dick Hoyt whose son was born with Cerebral Palsy? Imagine what people told him he could not do. Since 1977, he had been running marathons and competing in Iron Man contests. Then Dick decided to compete with his son by pulling him on a cart from his bicycle, swimming while pulling his son in a boat, and running while pushing him on a cart.

How about great leaders like Samuel M. Walton? He is said to have been one the greatest business leaders of all time – building one of the most powerful retail businesses in history. None of the people that are part of these great success stories were born with this skill or talent to achieve these great feats, but they all *became* great.

So, I challenge you as you read this book to decide what kind of leader *you* want to be and follow the key steps of belief, determination, and discipline to achieve your greatness.

BOOK STRUCTURE AND ORGANIZATION

If you are like me, most times when I have purchased or received a book I only get about halfway through it. Whether reading a great book by John Maxwell or any other great author, all too often I found myself getting too busy doing employee reviews, putting out fires, or just doing my daily job that I just could not finish the book. Then by the time I did begin reading the rest of the book, someone else would recommend another book to me, like *Good to Great* by Jim Collins. At some point, I found that I had read half of a lot of great books.

This book in your hand is written *by* a sales leader *for* the sales leader. Each chapter is designed to be read independently or along with the others. So, if you do not complete the entire book and choose to read only select chapters on sales leadership, you win!

When you see a
box like this, it
signifies an
important topic or
relevant quote.

More than anything, I wanted to make a book
that mentors would pass onto their protégés to
help them develop their leadership skills. What
you are going to read is not rocket science or
splitting atoms, but real life ideas that have
worked for hundreds of others.

*"No matter what your job is, you get paid to help people
and the more people you help, and the better you help them,
the more success* YOU *will achieve."*

1

SUCCESSFUL
LEADERSHIP

lead•er•ship (lē'der ship') n. 1. *an ability to lead.*

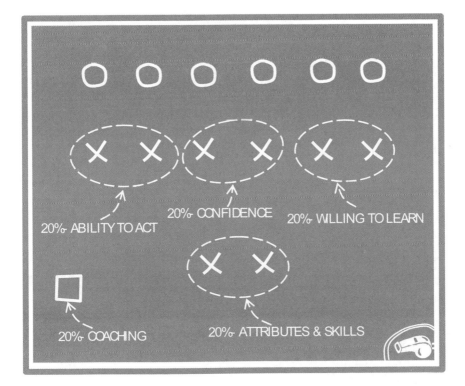

Great leaders from history continue to be remembered and quoted. We quote great government leaders, sports leaders, civil rights leaders, and business leaders. The success of these great historical leaders has been documented, and we have been studying them for years. So, then why do so many organizations continue to struggle with great leadership? Why does the ability to *excel* in leadership remain a challenge in corporations?

> If success is your ultimate goal there will be times you will have to "give up" a little something in order to practice to be the best.

My experience has shown that successful leadership does not come from simply reading and knowing what a great leader says and does. In fact, most leaders know *what* it takes to be a great leader, but simply cannot find the time, or know how to prioritize their time, to make it a way of life. Successful leadership can only be acquired from *doing it* and doing it *again and again*.

MAKE THE TIME

Becoming a successful leader requires time and persistence. Unfortunately, what we read about, learn, and want to implement all too often falls in the deep black hole of the many great ideas we never end up pursuing. *Sound familiar?* Perhaps you may have experienced this yourself – most of us have. Have you ever gone away on a leadership retreat or decided to use a great leadership book as the blue print of how your leadership team was going to improve? Then, six months later found yourself back to doing the same things you were doing prior to the retreat?

I remember attending a leadership retreat with my boss and all of my peers quite a few years back. We spent two days studying the book *'Top Grading'*. During the retreat, we discussed how we were going to align our teams and leadership style with this book. We even planned a number of great activities we would put into place to implement these programs. We left the retreat motivated to make the changes to better our teams and improve our leadership.

Three months after the retreat, our plans became a reference of what we were *going to do*. Then six months later, we never discussed them again. What happened? It is simple – we did not internalize and follow the success blueprint we were given. Unfortunately, I find this outcome is more the norm than the exception. All too often we forget that success depends on well planned, consistent behavior.

WRITE IT DOWN

I encourage all leaders to fill the black hole of *never implemented great ideas* with action. To succeed, you must stay on target to achieve your leadership goals. The first step to making this happen is to write down exactly what you want to do. This can often be the hardest step – so do it *immediately*. Do not wait for the time to be right, do not get ready to do it, and do not wait till Monday, the new month, or the new quarter to do it. *Just do it* – and do it now!

> Success depends on well planned, consistent behavior.

Yes, *just do it* was a slogan popularized by Nike, but it is also extremely useful in business. Many people and organizations are "fixin" to get things done, but never do because they feel the timing is not right. The reality is that, unless you make it a priority, the timing will never be right. You have to *want* to make it happen right now, and *just do it*.

BEING A LEADER: 20% - ATTRIBUTES & SKILLS

When we talked about Tiger Woods being the best golfer in history, and not a "natural born" golfer, it was with the understanding that we are born with some talents, while others are developed through hard work and dedication. However, if "natural born" talent is left untouched, it will just go away or fail to develop.

Tiger Woods tapped into his golfing abilities young and then had the *desire* (this being the actual talent he was born with) to go after it. He practiced – oh did he practice, and practiced some more. There were many days and nights when Tiger probably missed some fun activities with his friends because he had to be either resting or practicing, but he *chose* this – he *desired* to succeed.

Like Tiger Woods, many of us are born with the desire to succeed. Desire to succeed is just one of many *attributes* people are born with. Through valuable life lessons, we further learn and enhance our knowledge which strengthens our attributes. So, what exactly is an attribute?

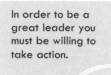

In order to be a great leader you must be willing to take action.

An *attribute* is defined as: *a quality or characteristic inherent in or ascribed to someone or something.* In laymen terms, an attribute is something that is inherently part of who you are as a person.

Key *attributes* that a great leader needs to possess include kindness, strength, discipline, focus, vision, action and self-motivation.

What are *your* attributes and how can you improve them to become a better leader? Take the time now to list three of the top leadership attributes you have and the ones that you would like to have:

I HAVE:

1.

2.

3.

I WOULD LIKE TO HAVE:

1.

2.

3.

Just because something is inherent does not mean practice is not required. As with anything worthwhile, to maintain and improve an attribute, you must put it into practice – into *action*, and consistently use it. For someone who does not inherently possess an attribute, they will need to first work to acquire it. Then, practice will be needed to develop and strengthen it.

SKILLS OF LEADERSHIP

A *skill* is something that *can be learned* and definitely not something we are born with despite what people say (we have been through this, and I think you understand). Key *skills* for a great leader include: communication, prioritization, delegation, coaching, the ability to get people to follow, the ability to create ownership in others, and the ability to teach others to be future leaders.

Communication skills allow a leader to communicate his vision to the team. *Successful* communication allows the team to understand the vision and goals and adopt them as their *own*. During tough times, a strong communicator will not sympathize with his team and console them; rather, he will guide them toward the winning path.

People must *want* to follow you on the path you have communicated, not just because the organizational chart says so. People will follow you as a leader if they believe you have the answers and knowledge needed to help them achieve their goals. This is a key requirement – it *must* be *their goal too.*

> In order for your team to own the vision, they must feel as if they contributed to it.

No one, no matter how dedicated of an employee, wants to be given an order and then told, "Now, go do it." This communication style leaves them without input or the ability to use their own skills and knowledge to achieve a task. When communicating with your team and getting them to follow you, make sure it is on a path that has been created together.

LET'S TALK ABOUT IT

How can you do this and still retain your leadership stance? Start by asking your team for their opinions – their visions. Be sure to stay on track and not let their input get *you* lost. In other words, you must know what the final destination is and what cost you are willing to spend, which is not always monetary. With your leadership and direction, let your team help make the road map to achieve their goals so that they *own* them and *desire* to achieve them. Use your action list to guide the process.

To reinforce this concept, I want to use a common, real-life scenario, which I am sure you have seen happen before. There are two teenagers. One teenager is given a car by Mom and Dad. The other teenager has to work, save and sacrifice for his car. Of these two teenagers, one babies the car like it could break any minute and takes great care of it. The other always forgets to wash it, change the oil, or even gas it. Which teenager do you think took care of his car and which one did not? The answer: the one who worked for it took care of his car. The reason why is because a vested interest leads to success. This same concept applies to individuals and goal setting. Let your employees own the goals, and they will care about achieving them.

> Vested interest from your team will lead to success.

As with most things, there are exceptions to this as a leader. There will be times when you are given marching orders from the top that must be precisely executed – times when what must be accomplished is not negotiable. In this situation, it is much harder to create ownership for your team. At such a time if you did ask for their ideas, but followed the orders anyway it could easily appear that you did not care enough to use their ideas. During times like this, I find it best to ask for help from your team to create ownership on the *atmosphere* of the marching orders. Gain their understanding, not just their ideas.

WORDS IN ACTION

In 2002, I took over a market and right away I was handling a budget issue with a large lack of return on investment. I had over 400 contracted sales people that were being paid extravagant amounts of money to sell a product with very little product being sold. I consulted the finance department about this specific problem and soon found out that this market spent the most dollars with the least amount of return in the country.

Based on the situation, I felt the best decision was to change the compensation structure in order to increase production. This was a time when I had to approach my sales managers who ran this department with marching orders, but needed their buy-in to help effectively communicate and execute the plan.

First, I explained to them the problem and showed them where we were headed if we did not fix it. Then, I asked for their help in executing the changes. Most importantly, I needed their help in creating a positive atmosphere around the changes (put more money in the commission and less in the salary, rewards for production, etc.) so that we could create a winning atmosphere around a perceived bad situation.

> If you can't gain total buy-in, gain total understanding by pointing out the path to success *or* failure.

Within the first week, we created the new compensation plan along with the new expectations for all of the employees in this organization (did you read the '*we*' part?). The first step was to take 30% of their current hourly wage and move it to their commission. The second step was to realign the leadership positions to maximize growth and profitability. This was done by having the twelve supervisors take on a coaching and training role and less administrative work by realigning their daily job duties and expectations. Then, we took the twenty-five senior sales people and put them in the stores to actually sell versus the training that they were previously doing.

Delivering this message was not an easy task, but getting everyone's buy-in was a must. During the roll out of the changes, the division manager explained the current situation and showed the team that, by making these changes with the team's help, the company and they would increase their results and profitability.

Not everyone agreed immediately (some even left right off the bat). But the core of the team started to work towards the goal and the others soon followed. Soon, the entire team was seeing the results and celebrating their new found success. Within twelve months, the contract labor team was number one in the country with the greatest return on investment and highest production.

BEING A LEADER: 20% - COACHING

A successful leader must be a *great coach*. A coach is a person that improves his team on a regular basis. No matter how good your team is they can *always* improve and learn.

Being a good coach means creating a culture of constant practice and improvement. While it is important to recognize your team's accomplishments, you should never become content. Even though most companies will agree that coaching is one of the most important skills to building a winning organization, most companies do not actually teach their managers how to coach.

> A successful leader creates a culture of constant practice and improvement.

Instead, when a person is promoted to manager, they are given sexual harassment training, employee review training, process training, etc. If an organization expects its managers to train and develop their employees, they must teach the managers how to be a coach. However, very few organizations have training to help managers learn how to be a coach.

BE WILLING TO TRAIN

The organizations which struggle the most are the ones that hold their training departments (or similar such departments or people) accountable for training and developing their organization instead of the direct manager. It may be the training department's job to create many of the curriculums, but is the leader or coach's job to teach and develop their team members.

A coach (leader), much like in sports, is the person who is responsible for making each team member better. Coaches must hold everyone accountable to expectations given. It is their job to skillfully identify and apply everyone's talents on the team. Lastly, a coach understands how to help individuals achieve their best performance.

When someone is managing rather than coaching, he or she will focus on people's weaknesses and try to help them improve their weaknesses while allowing their strengths to sometimes stay stagnant. A *great coach* will focus on the team's *strengths* and continue to push each individual to improve their greatest abilities in order to over compensate for any weaknesses. I am not suggesting you should completely ignore their weaknesses; they just should not be your focus.

WHO'S ON FIRST?

In baseball, there are people who are *designated hitters* or a great pitcher who cannot really hit. Coaches do not focus on making a great pitcher a better batter; rather they make them an even better pitcher. So, why do we feel the need to always focus on people's weaknesses in business? Let us explore how this affects the individual.

> A great coach will focus on the team's strengths – not their weaknesses.

We all love to do things when we are good at them. In fact, we are usually more willing to work on making these strengths even better than on diminishing our weaknesses, which we feel will never improve. Also, if we can focus on our strengths at work, then we typically experience complete job satisfaction. On the other hand, if we are constantly working or doing tasks that we are not very strong at and constantly feeling like a failure, we are not going to enjoy our job and will typically find a more rewarding fit elsewhere.

THE LINE UP

Just like everything in life, there must be a balance, and a good coach will put the right people in the right place working on the right job.

Team members who have a great coach are able to make the two following statements:

1.   My coach taught me new things last month.

2.   My coach has scheduled practices for the team and makes them a priority.

Ask yourself this question: what successful coaches, in any sport, did not teach their players something on a monthly basis or did not make their team practice? So, why should it be any different in business? Manager is simply a title, but *coach* is the *job* of a great manager or leader.

I encourage managers to *manage* the *business* and to *coach* their *employees*. To coach an employee means to practice with them on a regular basis by making their strengths stronger and their weaknesses less weak. Imagine a football team who never practiced field goals, but instead waited until game day to "try it." Consider a basketball team who never practiced free throws until game day, and then gave it their "best shot."

Remember, the best team does not necessarily win because they always execute the most difficult plays. Most of the time, they simply practice the "basics" along with the "tried and true" plays, and combined with these they get winning results.

BEING A LEADER: 20% - WILLING TO LEARN

> "Personally, I'm always ready to learn although I do not always like being taught."
>
> -- *Winston Churchill*

Have you ever worked with someone who absolutely knew it all? There was nothing you could tell or teach them because they had "been there, and done that." Certainly, you could not possibly know something they did not already know. If you want to be a great leader, then do not be that person.

You can always learn from your team, from your mistakes, and even from your clients or prospects. *Listen* as you do your job. Hear what your team is expressing. This does not mean that you listen to the moaning and groaning, which can sometimes arise during difficult times or from difficult people – this behavior must never be encouraged. Instead, listen to real concerns when your employees come to you with them.

OPEN DOOR, OPEN MIND

Here is one rule you can apply to this process: "When you come to me with your concerns, also come with solutions." This simple rule will put a stop to your team just *complaining* (there are perhaps better words for this, but I will keep it clean). In other words, before complaining, encourage your team to work through a possible solution (write it down even) before bringing the complaint to you. This will allow them to be more open to your suggestion and to finding a winning solution.

> Tell your team to develop possible solutions along with their concerns.

There is an old saying, "Everything alive is either growing or dying." The truth of this statement is something we all could live by and another great philosophy for business. Though many people say they want to learn, are they actually *willing* to learn? Winston Churchill once said, "Personally, I'm always ready to learn although I do not always like being taught." Churchill certainly was not alone; in fact, this statement rings true for most people in business today.

THROW IN THE TOWEL OR GRAB A TISSUE?

In 1998, I was conducting a one-on-one meeting with a manager of mine who was responsible for running one of my four sales teams. She was a very intelligent person and a good manager. She possessed over fifteen years of sales experience along with eight years of sales management experience. She truly cared about her work and wanted to learn. Unfortunately, she was very difficult to coach.

During our meeting, I attempted to bring up a skill she could improve on, which would help make her a better leader and prepare for her next step in her career. She became defensive with me and completely shut down. I overlooked her response the first time it happened, but after a few one-on-one meetings, which netted the same result, I began getting frustrated and thought I was making a mistake in trying to help this manager grow as a leader.

So, I decided to do a little research. I spoke with a couple of her previous managers who told me they found the same obstacle when they managed her and that they stopped trying to coach her. Both of her previous managers agreed she did her job well enough at her current level and had decided it was easier to not focus on developing her because she made it very difficult.

> Even difficult employees need and want to be coached.

In my next meeting with this manager, I asked her what her goals were in the organization and if she was looking to be promoted to the next level and grow as a leader. She responded excitedly, "Absolutely! However, I have been in the same position for over seven years, and I have not been asked to interview for the next level position during the past four openings."

I asked her what she thought about coaching and personal development. She eagerly answered, "Yes, I want someone to help me develop as a better leader!"

I nodded my head with understanding as I leaned back and grabbed a box of tissues off my credenza and got them ready. I knew this was not going to be an easy conversation, but I felt I owed it to this manager who was good. I wanted to help her.

I started off by explaining to her that if she *wanted* to be coached and get to the next level she had to be *willing* to be coached. I shared with her that I, along with her previous two managers, believed she was a great manager with some great potential to grow as a leader. However, coaching her appeared to be way too difficult.

As expected, she started to get defensive. I used her reaction as an opportunity to show her exactly what I was referring to and why some of her past managers (and almost I) had given up on her. At this point, I had captured her complete attention. I explained further how I would be willing to work with her, coach her, and then recommend her if she would be *willing* to learn.

After a two hour meeting and a few Kleenex tissues (emotions are not always a bad thing – sometimes it means passion and ownership for a job), she understood and was willing to be coached. Hooray!

In the end, I am very glad I took the time to work with her because, as she allowed me to coach her, I witnessed her growth. I also found myself growing and becoming a better leader too.

Be easy to coach or people will stop trying.

I almost did exactly what her previous managers had done, which was to not waste my time and energy on coaching her to be better because I felt it may not be worth the time and energy, and that it would be just too difficult to do. This experience taught me that everyone is worth taking the time needed for improvement and advancement.

STAY IN THE GAME

I live by the advice I give to many: "Be easy to coach or people will stop trying." Willingness to learn and change takes discipline, modesty, and, most of all, *hard work*. Think about it. It is much easier to continue doing things the same way you are doing them today than to have to take time to learn a new system. However, the gain from doing things the easy way is short-term.

What if everyone remained short-sided in their efforts? What if doctors and the medical community stopped being willing to learn and advance medicine? Would we still treat an infected wound by cutting off the patient's limb? No, of course not! We *expect* doctors and scientist to find new cures and treatments.

So, with that in mind, what is to be said about the leader who has been leading people the same way for the past 20 years? Are they doing a good job by today's standards?

Over the past decade alone, we have learned a lot about leadership and leadership skills. I encourage you to look back over what you have learned and what you have implemented to make you a better coach and leader. I challenge you to take some ideas and programs from this book, and implement them to improve your leadership today.

Being a Leader: 20% - Ability to Act

Take *action*, even if you make mistakes. Mistakes are a natural part of the decision making and learning process – remember this as you make every decision. I used to tell my teams, "If you are not making mistakes, you are not making enough decisions." The truth is unless you are a brain surgeon (or the like) no one is going to die because of a bad decision you make.

> If you are not making mistakes, you are not making enough decisions.

Take *calculated* risks. What is a calculated risk? Based on the information you have (that means you have to work to get as much information as you can), make an informative decision and then go from there. Numerous books have been written about executing a plan and getting the job done. Even Elvis had a slogan which he lived by: *TCB* with a lighting bolt – meaning: *Take Care of Business in a Flash*.

As a leader, one of my rules for my team was to call a peer some where in the country every week and share best practices. In every new team I would lead, when I first started asking my managers to do this, they often acted concerned and defensive. Some of them thought I must not believe what they were doing was working. So, I would have to explain to them that I wanted them to share best practices with their peers because they can learn from each other.

Once, a manager announced to me that he did not think we should share our best practices. He explained that, if my goal was for them to be number one, by sharing what they were doing, everyone would do the same things therefore preventing anyone from being number one. My response to him was this: "The difference that will make us number one is our discipline and ability to take action on the best practices."

There is a saying: *"Knowledge is power."* Well, I for one disagree. If that was the truth, then librarians would be the most powerful people. They have access to tons of knowledge contained within the pages of books (of course, this is not to say there are no powerful librarians in the world). However, knowledge is only power when you have the discipline and the motivation to do something with it. You must be willing to *take action*.

BEING A LEADER: 20% - CONFIDENCE

A leader must be *confident*. If a leader is confident, the followers will presume they are *competent*. There will always be times when a leader is not exactly sure of what to do. Whatever happens, the team should not feel this. Let them know when times are tough. Let them know you are reviewing options, but do not let them *feel* it. Always be *confident* in yourself, your team and your decisions.

If you got on a plane traveling from Los Angeles, California to Dallas, Texas, and, as you were walking onto the plane, you asked the pilot, "What do you think about our flight today?" And he responded, "Well, I *think* we will make it. I mean we have done it before." Do you think you would feel confident about his ability to get you to Dallas? I would say probably not. Perhaps you might feel compelled to run back up the runway and find another flight!

Flying Leap

Here is a true story about flying and confidence. In January of 2007, my wife and I were flying back to Dallas, Texas from a speaking engagement in Las Vegas, Nevada. We absolutely had to get to Dallas this same night because we had another speaking engagement at 8:00 a.m. the following morning. The weather in Dallas was terrible with severe ice storms and snow (it should be noted that winters are not normally too severe in Dallas; so, this was unexpected). All previous flights had been canceled and this flight was the last and only one out.

Before I go on, let me also tell you that, although my wife flies all over the country, she is terrified of flying. I mean *terrified*. She even takes a prescription medication in order to relax her enough to fly.

So, as the story goes, we begin to board the flight. Honestly, we really thought even this flight was going to be cancelled, but were grateful it was not. As soon as we reach our seats, the flight attendant gets on the intercom system and starts with this truly motivational speech:

> "Welcome to ABC airline. As you know, we *may* be the first flight to land in Dallas today (please note the key word being 'may'). Now folks, we cannot control mother-nature. So, please understand. And *hopefully*, we will arrive safely in Dallas."

What was she trying to say? Not only did her words sound terrible, but her tone, loaded with 100% doubt, assured us that we were doomed!

At this point, my wife is trying to grow wings herself and fly to Dallas. To make matters worse, the passengers next to us begin talking about how we might not make it too! As you can imagine, my wife was having a complete "come apart" (that is Texan for panic attack).

The pilot must have overheard this less than reassuring speech given by the flight attendant because soon thereafter his voice was heard resonating through the cabin.

With a calm tone, which emanated 100% confidence, he said:

> "Folks, thank you for flying ABC airline. I want to let you know we just came from Colorado and we are now going to Dallas. We will be flying above most of the weather; so, please relax and enjoy your flight. We don't expect any other delays and we will be landing in 3 hours and 30 minutes."

Now, I do not know how he felt inside, but he sounded very *confident.* Therefore, we felt that he was *competent,* which brought an end to the grumblings. In the end, the flight ended up being just fine with only a few bumps and an extra glass of wine for my wife.

This story clearly shows the impact a leader's confidence can have on his followers. Now, granted, we had no choice, but to follow because we were on his plane. However, we felt safe and assured that the pilot knew what he was doing.

Take a moment and think about the many ways a leader in the workforce affects their employees. First, they are responsible for their team's livelihoods. They also contribute to their job satisfaction and a major part of their overall success. So, how important is it that the leader be confident in their decisions and direction? The answer is – *very.* An employee must believe their leader is going to show them the way to success, so much so that their families are counting on it (that would be the paycheck they bring home). Confident leaders do not ignore their fears; they act in spite of their fear.

CHAPTER 1 HIGHLIGHTS

- Great leadership is a constant process.

- Coach the employees and manage the business.

- "Personally, I'm always ready to learn. Although, I do not always like being taught." – *Winston Churchill*

- Knowledge is only power when you have the discipline and the motivation to do something with it and take action.

- Confidence breeds competence. When people believe you are confident, they will believe you are competent.

2

SHARING THE VISION

vi•sion (vizh' en) n. 1. *an optimistic view of where the organization wants to be in at a set time in the future.*

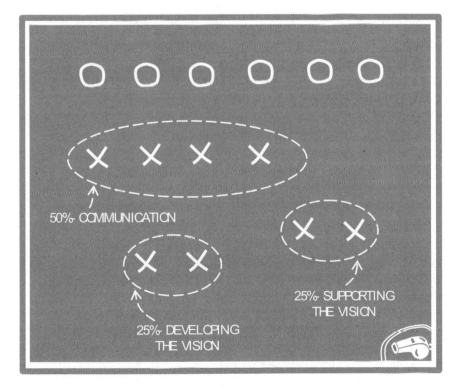

When creating a *vision*, a leader must have an understanding of where the organization is and where it needs to go. The vision of the business gives it energy. It helps motivate employees in the direction of corporate strategy. It is the image that a business must have of its goals before it sets out to reach them. It describes aspirations for the future, without specifying the means that will be used to achieve those desired ends.

> "Coming together is a beginning; keeping together is progress; working together is success."
>
> -- Henry Ford

A vision can be looked upon as the beginning of an organization's story. It creates purpose for the team by focusing them on what they need to work together on to achieve success. It includes the motivation and plan to encourage improvement and achievement.

BEING A VISIONARY: 25% - DEVELOPING THE VISION

The success of your vision is determined by how well it fulfills five basic requirements: provides future direction, expresses a consumer benefit, is realistic, is motivating, must be fully communicated, and consistently followed and measured.

A vision should be a short, succinct, and inspiring statement of what the organization intends to become and to achieve at some point in the future. The intentions listed in the vision should remain broad, all-inclusive and forward-thinking. While there are no specific formulas for creating a vision, there are principles and guidelines for building one. To begin the development of your vision, follow this simple three-step process:

1. Think of all the things that might be possible for your organization in a given time frame.

2. Write down as many ideas as you can.

3. Edit the list to what you are willing to commit to.

By going through this brain storming exercise, your mind becomes open to areas of new possibilities. This is essential to developing a vision because, after all, a vision is putting into words the goals and desires of the future which is a yet unforeseen state of existence.

Here are some examples of corporate vision statements:

- GE – We bring good things to life.

- Ford – To become the world's leading consumer company for automotive products and services.

- Microsoft – To enable people and businesses throughout the world to realize their full potential.

The more powerful and vivid your vision, the more opportunities occur to create the strategies necessary to your business success. Building a vision is actually only one part of the larger activity – developing the governing ideas for the enterprise, its vision, mission, and business plan. It is an essential starting point of building a winning team. A vision not consistent with values that people live by on a daily basis will not only fail to inspire enthusiasm, it will generate blatant criticism and cynicism.

BEING A VISIONARY: 50% - COMMUNICATION

Once developed, the vision must be supported and communicated to all team members. Surprisingly, many leaders develop a vision, which they believe to be the greatest vision for their organization, but find out that their employees are unaware of it. This result is not necessarily due to how the vision was created, but, instead, how it was *communicated* and *understood* by the members of the team.

In order to effectively communicate your vision for your organization, you must be able to explain the what, how, why, and when. By keeping your organization informed, you build trust which in turn empowers your team. Visions that are truly shared take time to emerge. They grow as a by-product of interactions and require on-going conversation.

There are four steps needed to communicate a vision:

1. Share your vision and how it will benefit the organization as a whole.

2. Show how the achievement of the vision will benefit each team member.

3. Share your plan of action as the leader including what each team member can expect from you.

4. Share your expectations of them.

Now, let us take some time to walk through each of these steps in better detail.

STEP 1: SHARE YOUR VISION AND HOW IT WILL BENEFIT THE ORGANIZATION AS A WHOLE

The creation of the vision combined with effective communication of the vision creates long-term success. Henry Ford said it best, "Coming together is a beginning; keeping together is progress; working together is success."

> The more a person understands something – the more they are willing to believe in it.

The more a person understands something the more they are willing to believe in it. Most people (and definitely all the people that I would want in my organization) want to be a part of something great. So, take the time to ensure every person understands the impact of the vision before going to the next step.

STEP 2: SHOW HOW THE ACHIEVEMENT OF THE VISION WILL BENEFIT EACH TEAM MEMBER

This step is huge. I know we do not like to admit it out loud, but people are self-centered. I do not mean that in a bad way – just in a *real* way. People work to make money so they can take care of the people they love the most – their families and themselves. When we are mindful of this fact, we can align what will benefit us with what will benefit the group or society. This is commonly referred to as a *win-win* situation, which is a very good thing.

In all my organizations, I always made sure to talk about how each person would individually benefit from the vision. For example, when I ran several retail stores, our vision was to offer first class customer service. I first asked my store managers this question, "If we do this, how would this impact your life?" Their response was positive. Then, I went into specifics and asked them, "How would it impact you as a manager and your employees if we decreased the number of upset or unhappy customers that entered your store by fifty percent?"

> Employees need to internalize the vision's personal benefits to them.

Their response was once again unanimously positive, "That would make our day and all our employees' lives better." They were pumped up and eager to hear more. So, then I asked, "What if our referral of new customers increased by twenty percent? By doing this, how would it effect the sales people's commission in the stores?" This one they really loved! They enthusiastically stated, "It would be great! We could assume that everyone's income would go up by an average of 15% – giving them three times their normal annual raise of 5%."

My conversation with them allowed my organization not just to hear about the vision, but, much more importantly, they internalized the personal benefits to them.

STEP 3: SHARE YOUR PLAN OF ACTION AS THE LEADER INCLUDING WHAT THE TEAM CAN EXPECT FROM YOU

In this step, I would share with the organization my personal business plan. In my plan, I stated my personal contribution to the team to ensure we achieved our vision. Now, they knew that not only would I hold them accountable, but they were to hold me accountable too.

STEP 4: SHARE YOUR EXPECTATIONS OF THEM

After you have communicated the vision and shared your plan, have your team create their own business plans to show you how they will put the vision into action. Their plans should be developed around exceeding your expectations. This topic is covered in detail in *Chapter 8* when we discuss how they are going to create their plans of action.

MORE THAN WORDS

Learning how to better communicate your vision can happen sometimes when you least expect it. This was reinforced by an event which recently occurred at my church.

My wife and I were sitting in the fourth row listening to Pastor John of our home church discuss the vision of the church. He discussed how the church had started just seven years ago with forty members and today we were expanding the church to handle a congregation of more than two thousand members. He then stopped and asked everyone in the congregation if anyone knew the church's vision.

The already quiet room became dead silent as people starting looking around to see if anyone was raising their hand to answer. After a few minutes (which seemed like a lifetime), the pastor, in his genuine way, let the congregation know that it was O.K. and that no one from the previous three services knew the vision either.

In fact, he went on to say, during his recent leadership conference he had with the church's leaders, no one there knew the vision either. The only person besides himself that knew the vision was his wife.

Now here is where the pastor showed his greatness. Unlike many business leaders, he did not blame the lower management (or the congregation) for not knowing the church's vision. Instead, he blamed himself. He told us that he thought the vision was either not as great as he first thought it was, or, more importantly, it was not correctly communicated. Either way, he wanted to fix it.

During this service he brought up his white board and markers (going outside the norm for many churches) and spoke to the congregation as a team. He had everyone get out a pen and paper and take notes. First, he started with the goal of the vision and spent the next twenty minutes breaking down the vision into four acronyms to help everyone remember. Next, he showed how *each person* in the congregation contributed to the four acronyms in order to achieve the overall vision. *Wow!*

I share this with you because, as a leader of several organizations, I have shared many vision and mission statements. Some were successful while others not, but, as I sat in my chair and watched the pastor, I realized what I had been missing, which I also believe most others in the business world today are missing too – the ability to take on the task of ensuring that the vision is clearly *understood*, not just clearly *communicated*.

> A vision has to be understood not just heard.

Most leaders will somehow communicate a vision or mission statement and then look for understanding. When it is not found, they will typically blame those that do not understand. *Do not do this.* Instead, look inside and see how you can break it down, create ownership and effectively communicate to your teams. This will help generate the buy in needed for the vision to succeed. The pastor did not change his vision, but he changed how he communicated it.

How often do we see a leader share a vision with their organization in a large auditorium with optimistic views and goals for the organization? Of course, the audience members cheer in support of their leader. But three weeks later, if you ask the entry-level manager or employee to share the company's vision with you, they typically do not have a clue what he actually said. They, without a doubt, do remember the hoopla, song, and dance.

Communicating the vision is the responsibility of all leaders in any organization. Always be willing to *inspect* what you *expect*. Talk to your team members, especially those employees three and four steps away from your position. Just like in business or life, it is not so much what you say, but how you say it. Whether a vision succeeds or fails has more to do with how it is communicated than the quality of the vision itself.

BEING A VISIONARY: 25% - SUPPORTING THE VISION

To energize employees to work towards and share the vision requires more than a sign on the wall. It is more than just telling your team what you (and they) need to do too. Nothing happens by magic. As their leader, you need to live the vision, be seen living it, and constantly communicating it to your team.

Your team must understand the vision – the reasoning of the vision. They must own the vision. Owning the vision is a natural process that evolves from genuine enthusiasm for a vision. Only then can the team *accomplish* the vision, and more importantly experience the *reward* of achieving the vision.

Many visions never take root and spread – despite having deep merit. Visions can only spread through the reinforcement of increased clarity, enthusiasm, communication, and commitment. As people talk, the vision grows clearer. As it becomes clearer, enthusiasm builds.

Enthusiasm spreads fastest by early successes in pursuing the vision. Success of the vision causes people to talk about it, which in turn brings better clarity to the vision thus generating more enthusiasm. And then the cycle repeats itself again.

Vision is long term. People need a "guiding light" to navigate and make daily decisions. Visions need to challenge people, evoke a feeling that draws people towards wanting to be a part of something quite special.

CHAPTER 2 HIGHLIGHTS

- Vision is an optimistic view of where the organization wants to be at a set time in the future.

- Show how the achievement of the vision will benefit each team member individually.

- Just like in business or life, it is not what you say, but how you say it. When it comes to an organization's vision, it's not the vision that will make the difference; it is the communication of the vision.

- "Coming together is a beginning; keeping together is progress; working together is success." – *Henry Ford*

- Visions can only spread through the reinforcement of increased clarity, enthusiasm, communication, and commitment.

3

CREATING A
WINNING CULTURE

cul•ture (kul'cher) n. 1. *the sum total of ways of living built up by a group of human beings transmitted from one generation to another.*

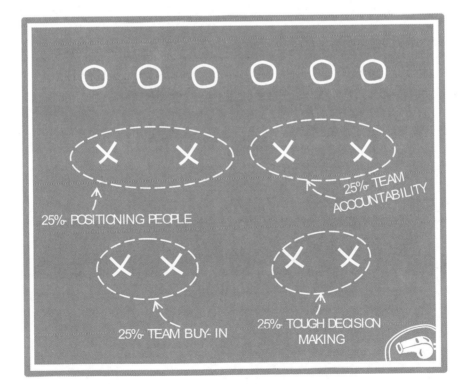

If leaders read only this chapter and none other, they will still be 100% better off than doing nothing at all. Creating a winning culture is probably the single most important aspect of success. In societies around the world, people's beliefs, ideas, laws and rules for conduct are created and developed by the culture of where they live. The culture of a society is one of the most powerful influences on a person.

I believe it to be the same in business today. A company's culture will determine the attitude, expectations and performance of their employees. Just like in the world, many companies have several sub-cultures within the same organization. It is up to the leaders of any organization to develop and nurture a thriving culture.

> Creating a winning culture is the single most important aspect of success.

Regardless of whether a leader develops one or not, a culture will be created in all organizations. The question I encourage you to ask yourself is, "What is my culture and who is creating it for my team?"

WINNING: 25% - POSITIONING PEOPLE

One of the first things a leader must do is to understand the team and its team members. Are the right people in the right positions? When making an assessment of a team and its team members, it is imperative to look at the character set of each employee. This is especially true when you are trying to place a new member within the team. Areas to consider include the employee's likes, attributes and skill sets.

All too often, we place employees in positions based on the organization's needs and not the individual's character set. Although this approach may fix a short-term issue with head count, the results are only temporary.

Over time, the ability for the team to deliver optimal results on a consistent basis will diminish because the team members were not placed in the best positions for them.

To understand the importance of positioning people better, let us break it down into three categories:

1. A person's interests or likes

2. A person's attributes

3. A person's skill sets

FIELD OF DREAMS

Imagine you are the manager of an electronics store and have an employee who happens to have a hobby of photography. Everyday when your employee comes into work, he stops at the digital camera area and moons over the equipment. Then, he slumps his shoulders and unhappily sighs as he makes his way to the computer department where he is assigned. Here is the question you must ask yourself, "Why would you not assign this person to cameras?"

> Passion for a job will equal the highest results.

All too often the answer is simple, "When I was hiring that person I needed a person in the computer department."

In the short term, having him in the computer department fills your immediate need. However, by taking the time to know about your employee and his interests, you discovered that he loves photography and knows all about the latest technology and techniques. Make it a priority to move people to areas where their talents can be best utilized. Enjoying their work makes them more valuable employees.

I have found that, when a person is working in an area where he has a great personal interest, he has more passion for it. This realignment will cause your employee to have a higher level of job satisfaction and in turn will typically deliver the greatest results. When this is done the employee is no longer working for a paycheck, he is working because he enjoys it. I like to say he is *plorking*, which means he plays for work and gets paid for doing it. This concept can be applied to every aspect of your business; people have areas of interest where they will flourish.

Keep in mind that just because someone has an interest in a topic or industry does not always mean they are going to excel at the position. In addition to having an interest, employees must have the right

Put the right people in the right place doing the right things.

attributes for the type of work they will be performing.

For example, I love to play golf and have a high-level of interest in golf. However, I am not a good golfer. In fact, one could say I stink (it's OK – most people I have played with have said it). Based on this skill set (or lack thereof), I will not be joining the PGA tour anytime soon. I lack some key attributes along with a lot of practice.

ATTRIBUTES

In order for a person to be successful in a position, they must have the right attributes for the job. Let us take a moment and examine the attributes for a sales person. A good sales person often possesses the following attributes: outgoing, energetic, confident, charismatic, self-motivated, humorous, focused, and persistent.

The hiring manager needs to understand what attributes the candidate for the position should possess in order to hire the best person for the job. Then, the manager must interview for those attributes before making the hiring decision.

When applying this process to a team that is currently in place, it works the same way. The manager needs to identify each position's attribute requirements and match them with the current team members.

The key is to be able to execute on this process regardless of how difficult it may be. By matching your team members' attributes with their desires, you are another step closer in creating a *winning culture*.

SKILL SET

The last piece to positioning people is *skill set*. I left skill set for the last topic because, although skills are very important, they can be taught and refined.

When identifying skill sets (as with attributes) it is important to understand what skill sets are needed for a position. For example, when I needed to hire someone as my executive assistant, I first identified that their likes and attributes met my needs. Next, I identified their skill sets. I knew I needed someone with strengths that compensated for my weaknesses. In particular, I wanted my assistant to possess strong grammar and writing skills, communication skills, organizational skills, multi-tasking skills, and the ability to make decisions and take action with limited direction.

> Your job is to get your team members in the right place – even if that place is outside of the company.

WINNING: 25% - TOUGH DECISION MAKING

There comes a point in the process when you realize someone may not fit anywhere. This is the time to make the decision that someone may fit better in a different position or department in the company, or even *another* company altogether. When this happens, it is your job to help them get there.

GO LONG

No one likes to have a job they are not good at. No one likes to feel that they are consistently performing below expectations. For example, there was an employee who had been working in the sales department for a long time, but who really just did not like working with outside people or with the pressure of quotas. As a result, the person regularly performed below expectations. However, the person really wanted to succeed. So, his poor performance had just been overlooked.

If you kept this person in that position, you would be doing this person a huge injustice. Help this person figure out what would be a better fit. It could be either a different department (IT, HR, etc.) or another company altogether.

Although he may not be receptive to changing at first (no one wants to be told he might work better in a different environment), he will truly respect you later when he is flourishing in the right environment. If you handle the situation correctly, everyone will appreciate your decision.

> We spend more time at work than home — we need to enjoy what we do.

By creating a short-term inconvenience of losing a team member, you will generate long-term benefit for both the individual and the team. Remember, we spend more time at work than we do at home. Everybody should be able to say they enjoy their work and feel they are successful. The effort taken by a strong leader to help the team realize what they really want moves them closer to achieving a *winning culture*.

RUN, PASS, PUNT

When I took over a sales team in 1996, I spent several weeks with each team member to identify what I thought and what they thought their attributes were. After my assessment, I met with each person individually and told them where they fit best in my new sales team.

As expected, not every conversation was a smooth one. As part of my assessment, I discovered several people were in jobs that did not allow them to be as successful as they could be. It was clear to me that, if they were in a different position or place, their jobs would become a rewarding experience.

I remember one young lady in a sales position who really did not like sales, which is probably why she had not obtained quota the previous six months. She did not enjoy prospecting and found that, regardless of the reports the previous manager had her complete, she very rarely prospected. She also did not deal with rejection well.

When I asked her if she would be willing to practice twice a week on role-playing prospecting and sales presentations, she said, "I would, but I would not like it. I don't think it would help me anyway." I appreciated her honesty, which just confirmed what I was going to do next. When I asked her how she liked her *job*, she responded that she liked the *company*, but did not like the feeling that she was going to get fired any day due to her performance. Based on my known history of turning over non-performers, her feelings were not unfounded. However, I thought she was a good employee doing the wrong job. Instead, I told her that I wanted to place her in a position she could succeed in and not have to feel like a failure everyday.

> Every day is draft day.

So, I moved her to customer service. It paid less money, but she enjoyed doing customer service, and she was good at it. Initially, she was very upset and disappointed because she felt like she was demoted. In truth, I did not demote her although she did take a pay cut. Instead, I took her from a position she was failing in and moved her to a position that she enjoyed, which matched her attributes and skill set, to ensure her success.

Six months later during a one-on-one meeting, she told me that although she was initially hurt and disappointed when I moved her to the customer service position, she was happier than she had ever been and enjoyed coming to work everyday!

EVERY DAY IS DRAFT DAY

There is value in each team member knowing that they are being evaluated on a regular basis. I am not just talking about the formal annual evaluations (although that is a good minimum starting point).

The NFL does a great job of this every year. Every year there is a new set of players coming to the team, and the existing team players have to earn their positions. Here are some good steps to follow:

1. When building a winning sales team, every day is draft day.

2. Always be looking for new and better talent. Be willing to make those tough decisions to replace current employees who do not share the same willing attitude.

3. Your team is valuable and everyone must understand it. Each person as an individual is important. Everyone must constantly focus on getting better at their job every day and winning the game.

4. A winning leader needs to care for his team members as much as each team member needs to care about the team and making it the best.

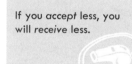

If you accept less, you will receive less.

To build this winning team, you must set the standards (and also expectations which are covered in another play). If you accept less than the standards, you will get less on a regular basis. Here is the list of standards for your winning team:

TEAM STANDARDS

1. A winning attitude – *always*. There will be tough days, but the attitude remains the same.

2. Each team member has the best attributes for the job. To know this you must list what you require for each job and make sure the team members have this.

3. Each team member must be a top performer in their position or getting better every day.

4. Each team member must practice.

5. The only failure is not to get back up.

6. Every team member must take ownership for themselves and their results.

7. Everyone shows support and respect.

Now that we have identified the right people, and the team standards, it is imperative to our winning culture that we coach each member to capitalize on their strengths and constantly get stronger.

WINNING: 25% - TEAM ACCOUNTABILITY

A popular belief is: focus on your faults to improve them. To this I say, "No! Focus on your *strengths* and capitalize on them." This idea should not invite you to ignore your weaknesses (or 'challenges' as we now like to say). Instead, place the *focus* on your strengths, your interests and likes; then apply them in business.

> Don't focus on the bottom performers – play favorites and spend time with the top.

I subscribe to the theory that a person is willing to work harder at improving on their strengths than focusing on their weaknesses. Consider this, if you spent three hours of your working day on a task (or a skill) that you did poorly, then most likely you would go home feeling like a failure and would find yourself with a very low level of job satisfaction.

However, if the opposite were true and your strength was, for example, presentation skills and you were asked to focus three hours a day improving your presentation skills and you enjoyed presenting, you would improve faster. Since you enjoyed it and you were good at it, you felt a great sense of success and accomplishment and worked even harder. This process requires a high level of accountability in order for it to work properly.

PET THE RACE HORSES AND KICK THE PONIES

As leaders and coaches, it is imperative to hold ourselves and our teams to the highest standards and results. As a leader, I spent the majority of my time with my top producers and "up and coming" superstars. I created a culture that to get attention and focus from the leader one must become a top producer or be willing to do what it takes to become one. I called this my *Pet the Race Horses and Kick the Ponies* theory.

All too often, sales managers tend to spend most of their time with the bottom 25% rather than the top 25% of their team members. It is felt that by working hard with the bottom performers they will improve thus increasing overall sales results. *This is a great way to not achieve the desired results.* Let us look at how the numbers work:

> The bottom 25% of your team performs and contributes 100 sales per month (put in any number you want). If you focus on them and increase this 10% you will get 10 more sales.

> The middle 50% continuously contributes 200 sales per month. This group will naturally increase a small percentage of 5-10% giving you an additional 10-20 sales extra per month.

> The top 25% contributes 400 sales per month. You focus on this group and get a 10% return and your increase is 40 extra sales per month.

You do the math with your group and you will see. Spending time with the low performers will cost you money (and more importantly your time) and still result in less production and revenue.

> Spending the majority of your time with low performers will cost you time and money.

Success like gravity flows from the top down through the ranks. By focusing on top producers, you are creating a culture that focuses on winners and those willing to learn and do what it takes to be winners. This will send a message to those who do not want to do what it takes or do not produce the desired results that they need to change or be left behind.

As a sales leader, I would spend the majority of my time coaching, training and conducting joint sales calls with my top sales people and my future top sales people. I would spend considerably less time with those that did not have the desire or discipline to be the best. Sometimes a team member would tell me I play favorites.

To this complaint, I would respond by saying, "You're right. I spend the majority of my time with the team members that are doing what it takes and have the desire to be better. If you want to be in that group, you must earn it."

By responding this way, I found that I would get the person to make one of the following decisions:

    a.   they would ask what it takes to get there and strive to be in the group, or

    b.   they would decide that they were not willing to do what it takes to be on a winning team and would choose to find an environment that met their lesser desires.

The results of this approach proved successful every time. After several months in a new market (I tended to be put in new or challenged markets), I was no longer the only one holding the team members accountable – peers would hold each other accountable.

WINNING: 25% - TEAM BUY-IN

The advantage of team *buy-in* comes when the leader is no longer the only one holding the team members accountable as stated earlier. The steps to achieving *buy-in* when creating a winning team are:

    1.   Share with the team the environment you are creating today. Let them know your plan for creating a winning environment.

2.   Show the results and the rewards of the environment. We call this WIIFM, which stands for "What's In It For Me?"

3.   Obtain the team's commitment.

As a leader, it is your job to put the desire and confidence back into each team member. This starts with putting the right people in the right positions, coaching them to excel at their strengths, and holding every member accountable to exceeding their expectations and contributing to the overall success of the team's culture.

CHAPTER 3 HIGHLIGHTS

- Cultures create beliefs, ideas, laws and behaviors.

- Put the right people in the right place doing the right things.

- The right person is based on a person's interest, attributes and skill set.

- "Pet the Race Horses and Kick the Ponies" theory.

- Every day is draft day.

4

TRANSFORMING A BELIEF SYSTEM

trans•form (trans 'fòrm) v. 1. *To change the form of; to change in appearance.*

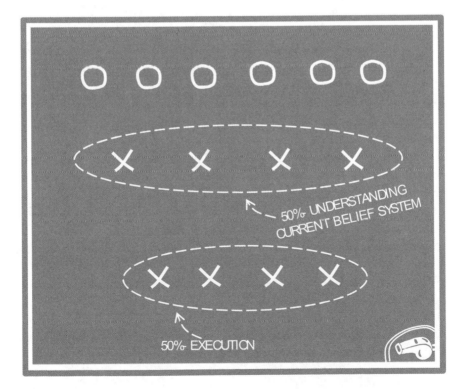

Belief systems provide a core set of values on which we base everything we do, say, or believe. A business's belief system sets the precepts from which it conducts its business, those which govern its planning, direction, and actions. Without these precepts a business could not function.

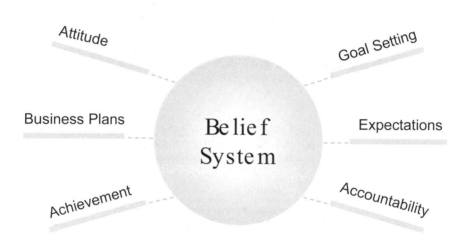

As depicted in the diagram above, the belief system is the nucleus of the organization and of a winning team environment. With the correct belief system in place, you can build everything from it. The belief system determines your team's attitude, which in turn determines your team's success.

The problem that we all run into from time to time is that our systems will fail us if we do not adjust them as we grow. It is much like an old pair of "lucky" socks that an athlete began wearing in little league. By the time he is in professional baseball, while those socks might have helped him when he was young, they have become full of holes and are way too small to do him any good. To continue winning games, he must be willing to reassess the value he placed on his lucky socks. As leaders, we must do the same. We must analyze our core values to see if those rules of old still fit our current business and direction. Before a leader can transform results, he must first be willing to transform the belief system.

However, it is during times of change that we may experience doubt and fear. We fear the unknown because we are venturing outside of what we previously set-up as boundaries for our safe harbor, or "business as usual." At this moment of change, we might feel lost if we do not have a new belief to put in its place. Overcoming the fear of change involves accepting that a belief system will change over time and taking control of the change so that it occurs at our pace.

VICTORY BELONGS TO THE MOST PERSEVERING

In the early spring of 2005, I attended a year-end corporate event with my team. At this event, we were being recognized as the number one team in the nation. When we arrived at the event, we were directed to a huge auditorium filled with over one thousand of my co-workers from across the country. The key note speaker was an artist. He came on stage, walked over to a painter's easel, and, as he began talking to us, he started to paint.

He continued painting while talking to us about creativity and belief systems. Several of my managers started rolling their eyes because, since the first day I met them in 2002, we have been talking about creating a winning belief system.

> At what age did we stop believing in ourselves and start believing what other people told us we could and could not do?

He began by sharing a story that put it so clearly. He told us about how he went to his child's kindergarten class and asked the children who in the room could paint really well. All of the children raised their hands. He then visited an eighth grade classroom and asked the students the same question, "Who in this room can paint really well?" This time only half of them raised their hand.

Next, he went to visit a college class of students and asked the same question, "Who in this room can paint really well?" Of the entire class of college students, less than 10% raised their hand.

Then, he looked to the crowd and asked us, "At what age did we stop believing in ourselves and start believing what other people told us we could and could not do?" This question made perfect sense to me. The answer was so clear: we stop believing because other people influenced us in some way that caused us to believe otherwise. This concept demonstrates how our belief systems are created.

The real challenge becomes deciding who we allow to create our belief system for us. Belief systems affect goal-setting, accountability and achievement of the team. If a team really believes in their ability and goals, they will hold themselves accountable to higher expectations. They will achieve greater results. Although it takes a lot more than a belief system to be number one, you will never be number one until you have a belief system to guide you.

> You will never be number one until you have a belief system to guide you.

Belief systems influence and shape businesses and business plans. If a team's beliefs are limited, their plans will tend to be conservative and yield lower expectations thereby delivering lower results. If the beliefs of a team are unlimited, the business plan will be more optimistic and aggressive yet still be realistic or obtainable.

Now that we know what a belief system is and its importance in determining our success, we must now learn how to understand and identify belief systems so that we can define and change them.

TRANSFORMING: 50% - UNDERSTANDING THE CURRENT BELIEF SYSTEM

There is a reason that the same leaders and sales people are at the top or quickly find their way there. It starts with their *belief system*. A *belief system* cannot be faked, although many will try and fail.

In order to transform a belief system (much like trying to stop an alcoholic from drinking), you must first *understand* the current belief system. We must figure out how it was created and why.

Once we understand it, we can then *identify* the areas of the current belief system which are hindering results and most likely job satisfaction. Once identified, these will be the areas targeted for change or elimination.

YOU CAN'T STEAL SECOND BASE AND KEEP ONE FOOT ON FIRST

In 2002, I was a Sales Director in California. During a sales meeting with my management staff, I shared my vision for our team to become number one in the country within twenty-four months. Before I could say anything more, a sales manager spoke up and announced that Southern California could never be number one in the country. He reminded me that the size of the market was too big. He further added that they had always been at the bottom, but they felt they understood why and were OK with that as a team. Does this sound familiar?

In this instance, they used their past results to justify their failures and determine their future. Whether he realized it or not, his comments set the stage for my next action – changing the belief system. I told my managers that the reason Southern Californian market was not number one was because they did not allow themselves to be number one. The size of the market was being used as an excuse to fail and had nothing to do with their real ability to be successful or not.

> "Do you want to be safe and good, or do you want to take a chance and be great?"
>
> -- Jimmy Johnson

The room went silent as I had expected. At this point, I started sharing with them my new vision. I explained to them what it would take to be a leader on this winning team. Many heads were nodding while others, including the manager who had spoken up, remained still.

Within the following ninety days after the meeting, I had two managers decide to leave the organization on their own. The only possible encouragement for their departure came from the new belief system I had laid out. Think about that for a moment – they wanted to leave because the pressure of striving to be number one was greater than their belief that they could actually be number one.

Did their decision prove that they were bad managers? Not really – they just were not able to change their belief system. They could not change their old belief that the Southern Californian market could never be number one. By being *unwilling* to change this belief, they were *unable* to do the things needed to make the market successful. To them, it was all a waste of their time.

On the contrary, the remaining managers grasped at this new belief system. In fact, they became part of the hiring process for the replacement managers to ensure they would be able to fit the new winning culture. Due to the remaining managers and the all new managers grasping the new belief system, in addition to understanding that the past did *not* predict the future, the market did indeed become number one in 2004.

ARE YOU IN OR ARE YOU OUT?

Performance is a key indicator of a belief system. Unfortunately, many leaders find themselves so busy with other "more important" matters that following-up on their team can often seem impossible. In the case of a team member who is saying "all the right things," it might even appear unnecessary. However, if the team member, who always says the "right things," has consistently low numbers, further probing is *required*. More likely than not, what this person says to you is not what they say to others. This is cancerous and must be addressed.

> Performance is a key indicator of a belief system.

This issue is commonly referred to as the *savior syndrome*, which is found all too often within middle management in sales. The *savior syndrome* happens when a manager places himself as the person who will protect his team from the "big bad" company. Oftentimes, a manager will do this in an effort to make himself feel important to the team thus increasing his value to the team. The manager starts by becoming more like a friend with the employees than their leader or manager.

As the team members become loyal to the new friendship, they become more willing to comprise their beliefs in an effort to protect their friendship. This behavior delivers a lack of accountability and low production. More importantly, it undermines any, and all, direction coming from the leaders of the organization thus making it impossible to achieve a positive belief system.

> The leader's responsibility is to be the person the team looks up to for success strategies.

One must remain in the leadership/manager role in order to create validity and success for the team. The leader's responsibility is to be the person the team looks up to for success strategies. The friendship/buddy system dilutes the strength and power of the leader. The team cannot succeed under this system. People are drawn to strong organized leaders. Be that person!

You must always look intently for the obstacles which might impair your ability to transform your belief system; they often appear where you least expect them.

MOST PEOPLE TAKE THEMSELVES OUT

Like many of the lessons I learned in my career, I learned this one from doing it wrong the first time. Then I allowed myself to be coached and taught by one of *my* leaders to recognize my mistake and fix it. At one point in my career, the company I was working for realigned some teams in the organization and in doing this I inherited an additional team. I did not mind the additional responsibility because it gave me a great sense of accomplishment.

Immediately after it was announced, I met with one of the newly placed managers to inform him that he now reported to me. We had known each other for over twelve months, but he had never reported to me directly until this point. This manager had been managing sales teams for over fifteen years and was not a rookie.

We discussed his team and his results, which were good, but not great. We talked about the difference between the environment he had been in and the environment of our present team. He assured me that he understood our environment and believed in it. He confirmed that he and his team would line-up and get onboard.

The new work and training schedule was more aggressive and expectations were much higher. However, during our first meeting, and our meetings thereafter, this manager told me everything I wanted to hear – he would have all the right information when I asked.

What I did not realize was that he had trained his team on how to respond to questions I would ask them about training and coaching sessions they had with him. About six months had passed, and, although I heard all the right things from him, his team's numbers were not lining up. I happened to mention my concerns with a former leader of mine, and he advised me that, if I went digging, I would probably find the truth. I assured him that he was wrong – this manager was getting it. It had to be something else.

> "I believe managing is like holding a dove in your hand. If you hold it too tightly you kill it, but if you hold it too loosely, you lose it."
>
> -- Tommy Lasorda

A few days later, I happened to get an opportunity to do a field ride day with one of the sales representatives on his team. We started a conversation about how things were going. He responded positively and told me he thought everything was going good. After we spent about six hours together that day, I asked him how the training was going. Before he could say anything, I glanced over at him and noticed his "deer in the headlights" look. Suddenly, he opened up and the truth came pouring out.

He admitted that he had not received training from his manager, and that his manager was, in fact, protecting him and his team from all of the requirements that the company and I were asking of them. Over the next few days, I dug further into the situation and discovered that this manager was saying one thing to the leaders and then telling his people the exact opposite. As it turned out, he alone was responsible for causing his team to struggle and contradict the goal and belief of the entire organization.

Needless to say, within the next month, the manager found a new opportunity outside the company. What lesson did I learn from all of this? I learned that the belief system has to be *real* to everybody. The leader needs to ensure that *everybody believes it.* As an end note to this story, the new manager, who took over the sales team, fully embraced the belief system, and the sales for the team increased by 40% over the following six months.

> The belief system has to be *real* to everybody.

HOME PLATE DOESN'T MOVE

As shown with the California market story, a leader must instill in his team that the past teaches us lessons, which we must apply to our future. The past does not, however, *predict* the future. Rather than let past performance limit you, use it to show you how great the future can be.

This belief can be tricky because a bad year, month or even day can damage a belief system. As the leader, you must be the rock of confidence during difficult times – for surely they will come. Your show of strength and determination will allow your team to regain their foothold on the belief system, and your boat will remain steady even in stormy waters.

TRANSFORMING: 50% - EXECUTION

When it comes to execution, you can only say, *Just Do It* so many different ways. However, as we have said several times and preach daily, "It is not what you know; it is what you do." Our belief system is no different. The belief system must become internalized. It must be used consistently on a daily basis in order to reach the goals that have been set. We must first believe. Then, we must become disciplined and focused enough to *execute* what we believe.

To help you gain a better understanding of this concept, I will share some different belief systems, which I have executed for myself and the teams I have led.

BELIEF SYSTEM #1: WE CAN BE NUMBER ONE

To start a change of an entire belief system, we would first establish a belief that we could be number one, and we were willing to do whatever it took legally and ethically to achieve our goal. Then, we identified the results or production we needed to support our belief. Finally, we determined what activities we would have to implement to achieve those results. This is very simple in concept, but NOT as easy to achieve. This belief system change required accountability of the leaders and the team. The reason the belief system was able to change from CAN'T to CAN was the execution of the belief.

> "Leadership is a matter of having people look at you and gain confidence, seeing how you react. If you're in control, they're in control."
>
> -- Tom Landry

During the early stages of the change, there were rumors floating around the office that there was a black list. The black list was supposedly a list of people who were heard or seen passing negative energy and infecting the team with bad morale. This rumor was true to a certain extent. The other leaders and I asked the team to hold each other accountable to our new belief of winning and being the best. If someone was creating bad morale, we wanted to know who they were so we could fix the morale issue.

When someone was identified, we met with them to understand why they were acting in such a negative way and why they did not believe in the team. Most would deny it, but, by confronting those employees, the team knew that having a bad attitude was not an option. In order to be a member on a winning team, each team member had to have the correct belief system. The big "stir up" only lasted for the first couple weeks because we addressed it openly and quickly. In the months to follow, we were free from this issue.

Change is difficult in all situations. It is even more so when you are dealing with hundreds of employees and something as large as a belief system. It took the entire team, not just one person, to change the belief system.

> "One of the greatest discoveries a man makes, one of his great surprises, is to find he can do what he was afraid he couldn't do."
>
> -- Henry Ford

So, allow me to ask the question, "Doesn't everyone want to be number one?" Those that say they do not care about being the best and just want to do a good job are the ones who have accepted the fact that they cannot be number one. Somehow, and at sometime, they have been discouraged or told they cannot be number one in their life and career. Sadly, they changed their natural born expectations to succeed to accept a more limited outlook on life. Someone has got to be number one – why not you?

BELIEF SYSTEM #2: GET HAPPY OR GET OUT, BUT GET SOMEWHERE

To ensure success, a leader has to make tough decisions about employees who may have talent and skills, but are holding the team back by their lack of belief. A good leader must be willing to make the decision to help change the employee or change their employment.

Another saying we have used to help identify a team belief system was, "Get happy or get out, but get somewhere." We said this because life is too short to do something we do not enjoy. Look at the facts – we spend over half of our time at work. The good news is that there are many places we can work. So, it makes sense to do something we like and enjoy it.

In order to meet our performance goals, we knew it would take all of our energy and focus. We could not get there if our key players were unhappy or did not have the same belief system. A team or group can achieve almost anything if they are willing to create a plan and execute that plan. Being the best is not easy and requires hard work. So, we must be willing to work hard. As both a leader and teammate, we must be willing to hold each person accountable and be held accountable ourselves.

ATTITUDE IS IMPORTANT

Bringing about change in people or in organizations is not simple. To make or break a belief takes commitment, and commitment comes from involvement. Involvement is the key to making change and increasing success. Of course, the downside of involvement is risk. Anytime you involve your team in the problem, you stand the risk of losing control. However, the rewards are worth this risk.

When people are meaningfully involved, they willingly commit the best that is in them. Once you as a leader have identified your team's belief system, with the involvement of your team, it is up to you to enforce it. This means not allowing people to discount the belief system or cause doubt in others. If the belief system is to motivate everyone and focus on positive energy, then you must begin by putting into practice what you say by holding others accountable and being accountable yourself.

By getting people involved in the problem, we build trust and accountability. Further, when your team identifies their personal beliefs with the beliefs of an organization, they produce an enormous amount of energy, creativity and loyalty.

CHAPTER 4 HIGHLIGHTS

- Leaders must transform the belief system before they can transform the results.

- At what age did we stop believing in ourselves and start believing what other people told us we could and could not do?

- It takes a lot more than a belief system to be number one, but you cannot be number one until you have the belief system first.

- The *savior syndrome* produces a lack of accountability and low production.

- Someone has to be number one – why not you?

5

PRACTICE MAKES PROFIT

prac•tice ('prak tes) v. 1. *To exercise one's self in, for improvement,*
or to acquire discipline or dexterity;

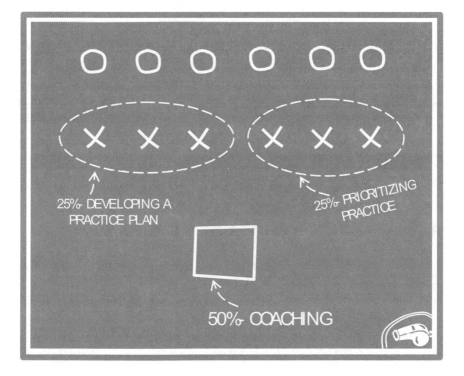

Sports teams and athletes spend 90% of their time practicing and 10% of their time playing the game. In sales, however, we spend less than 1% of the time practicing and 99% of our time playing the game. If a successful sales team requires the same elements that make up a successful sports team (like a great leader, drafting the best players, teamwork, positive mental attitudes, etc.), then why are we overlooking the most important element – practice? Think about that for a minute and ask yourself this question, "How high could your sales increase if you were to put a practice system in place?"

In sales today, I find most companies like to talk about training or practice, but do not actually do it. Of course, we need to be realistic – we cannot practice 90% of our time and also achieve our goals. It is just not feasible. However, we could implement a regular practice schedule. With regular practice, not only can one achieve given goals, one can *overachieve* them.

Before going any further, I want to make sure I am being clear. I have helped hundreds of companies implement a practice program over the past decade. These practice programs include weekly, monthly, and quarterly sessions. When I refer to practice, I mean actual *practicing* – not training. The practice that sales teams need should be focused on improving their selling skills and sales leadership skills. This is different from learning a new product and how it works. By setting aside time for your sales teams to practice, they will improve their skills and their numbers – practice *will* make profits.

PRACTICE: 25% - DEVELOPING A PLAN

> "Don't be afraid to give up the good to go for the great."
>
> -- J.D. Rockefeller

When I was an executive over the Indirect Retail Sales division of a major telecommunications company, I announced to my sales managers that we were going to initiate a team-wide practice program. The practice program would focus on negotiation skills, training skills, selling skills, and role-playing. I asked my sales managers to have a 45-minute practice session every week with their sales people as part of this new development program. I also asked groups of two to three of my sales teams to get together monthly in order to practice with each other for two hours. Then, once per quarter, my entire team would meet and practice together for eight hours.

For the quarterly practice sessions, I asked all of my managers to work together to create the practice schedule, which would help take our entire team to the next level. Quarter to quarter, most of the topics were not changed – we regularly focused on negotiation skills, training skills, selling skills, and role-playing. Our goal was *making excellent* the same skills, thereby, taking our team to the next level.

> Don't just practice; implement it into your daily work life.

Within two years of implementing the program, our division became number one in the nation. I attribute much of our success to the constant focus the managers and sales people placed on developing a practice program and executing this program daily. In other words, not only did they participate in the practice sessions, they actually implemented what they learned into their daily work lives.

PRACTICE: 25% - PRIORITIZING PRACTICE

I consider it interesting how we all believe that if you really want to improve at *playing* golf you *must practice*. Some people will even tell you that you will need a professional trainer or coach in order to become better. For those of us who are parents, we encourage, if not demand, our children to practice (I know I instruct my five-year-old step-daughter to *practice* her soccer skills so she can *improve* her playing).

Also, when we are sitting in our comfortable chairs watching a sporting event on TV, we often comment on how a professional athlete is not playing up to his normal standard (and does not deserve the money he is making) because he did not practice during training camp. Yet, in sales, we must master one of the most difficult skills in any industry, and we practice the least.

GIVING YOUR BEST IS NEVER REGRETTABLE

Some people are shocked when I remark that salesmanship is one of the hardest skills in any industry. The fact is that salesmanship is an art form comprised of intangibles like attitudes, egos, emotions, and energy. Great salesmanship requires discernment and the ability to adapt to situations beyond the control of the sales person.

It is not by coincidence that the sales departments of most companies have the highest compensated employees. Although, the steps required to sell are relatively simple, selling itself is not easy. Yet, most sales teams are not given the opportunity to practice once a month if even once a year.

> "Salesmanship, too, is an art; the perfection of its technique requires study and practice."
>
> -- J. C. Penney

Imagine if a professional sports team, like the Dallas Cowboys, used the corporate sales "practicing strategy." Players would practice the first week of their first year and never practice again. The coach would say, "Troy Aikman does not need to practice. He has been throwing the football since he was a kid; and he has been playing football for the Cowboys for 8 years. I just leave him alone and let him do his job on game day."

We would think the head coach had lost his mind. And after having a season of losing every game, he would get fired. Although this example might sound crazy, many corporate sales leaders have, when asked about training their sales people, said to me, "Oh, Nathan, most of my sales people have been here over 10 years and have been selling for more years than that." This might be true, but here is a fact: whether a person is a golfer, football player, or sales person, everyone must continue to *practice* to *improve* and to *win*.

HIT THE GROUND RUNNING

A sales practice program is not difficult to create. However, it will take great discipline and coaching to make it a long-term and effective program. A successful sales training program should address relevant sales topics such as prospecting, selling, negotiating, contracts, and presentation skills.

"Perfection is not attainable, but if we chase perfection we can catch excellence."

-- *Vince Lombardi*

If you choose not to implement anything else except this program in your organization, you will double your sales and most likely the income and attitude of your sales team.

Using selling and prospecting skills as an example, here is a sample curriculum:

SELLING AND PROSPECTING TRAINING CURRICULUM

1. Understand what the basic skills for your organization are (keep this simple)
2. Prospecting
   a. Tele-prospecting
   b. In-person cold calling
   c. Past or current clients
3. The steps of influential selling skills
   a. Build rapport
   b. Understand the customer's needs
   c. Map solutions
   d. Consideration (overcome objections)
   e. Ask for the sale

The curriculum should be developed using a combination of lecture, hands-on, and role-playing techniques. Concentrate on practicing each skill for two weeks.

At this point, the question arising in your mind is likely this, "How can I conduct weekly training sessions with my sales team? I need them out selling!" The answer is simple – Turn your sales meetings into a team practice. Here is how it would work using Tele-Prospecting as the example:

> On the morning set aside for your sales meeting, only spend forty minutes training and the remaining time recognizing top performers, providing company and team updates, and discussing topics in a round table format. Be certain to keep the discussions on track focusing on ideas and obstacles related to tele-prospecting along with role-playing a variety of scenarios.

Here is a sample sales meeting agenda:

TELE-PROSPECTING TEAM PRACTICE SCHEDULE	
8:00 AM	"Traveling Trophy" Weekly Sales Recognition for the Top Rep
8:10 AM	Tele-prospecting training (*How to effectively tele-market to target clients*)
8:50 AM	Company and Team Updates
9:05 AM	Round Table Discussion
9:15 AM	Meeting Adjourned

> Once the session is adjourned, take the teams newly practiced skills to the phones and conduct a 'dialing for dollars' morning. As your team's coach, you should be in the field with them – alternate between making your own calls and listening in on their calls. Give them feedback, encouragement, and push the energy up!

During your one-on-one meetings that week, discuss each team members prospecting efforts. Follow this program for two weeks per skill. At the end of the two weeks, go to the next skill. Never stop – keep practicing. If you focused on ten skills, and spent two weeks on each skill, you and your team would work on each skill two and one-half times per year. The benefits will add up.

PRACTICE: 50% - COACHING

Never assume that someone who was a great sales person will be a great sales coach. Coaching is a skill, much like selling, but, as a whole, many companies do not teach their managers how to coach. Instead, they teach them how to manage.

Typically, a new manager will attend HR training to learn about sexual harassment, disciplining employees, work place safety, etc. Although this training is important, it is less about making the team better and more about keeping the company from being sued.

> "Coaches who can outline plays on a black board are a dime a dozen. The ones who win get inside their players and motivate."
>
> -- *Vince Lombardi*

Instead, I encourage you to focus on developing a complete leadership program. One which will equip your new managers with a comprehensive skill set including handling HR issues, coaching, motivating, giving feedback, addressing conflict, planning, budgeting, effective street days, building team empowerment, and creating a winning culture.

Develop a schedule for practicing coaching with managers similar to the one designed for practicing sales. Although the skills and topics covered will be different, the same structure can be used.

WHEN IN DOUBT, PUNT

I found the key to building winning sales teams is more like building a winning football team and less like managing an office. In business today, we cannot control the economy, competitive pressures, and whatever bad news the media is talking about. However, we can control our selling skills and how good we are as leaders and sales people.

Remember, as with everything else on this planet, you are either growing or you are dying. Just because someone has been doing a job for a long time does not mean they cannot improve.

Despite the sport and business commonalities, as a sales professional or sales leader, we do not get paid to *play* a game, we get paid to *work*. You owe it to yourself, your family, and your team to practice and achieve the financial and morale success you deserve.

CHAPTER 5 HIGHLIGHTS

- Sports teams spend 90% of the time practicing and 10% playing the game. In business, we spend less than 1% of the time practicing and 99% playing the game.

- Selling is simple, but not easy.

- Replace weekly sales meetings with weekly practice meetings.

- Sales is one the most difficult skills.

- Just because someone has been doing a job for a long time does not mean they cannot improve.

6

SETTING CLEAR EXPECTATIONS

ex•pec•ta•tion (ek spek 'tā shen) n. 1. *That which is expected or looked for.*

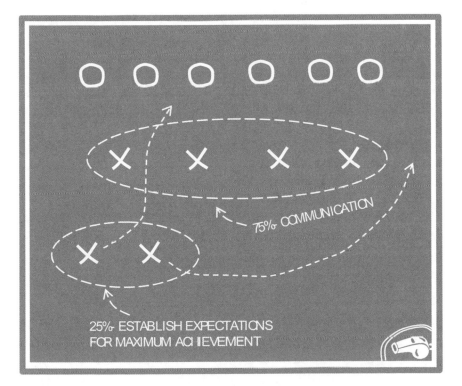

One of the major causes of problems which managers face today is unclear expectations between them and their team. Differences in expectations occur all the time. Whether it is personal or business related, each one of us enters into new relationships with certain expectations, which come from our previous experiences, roles, or relationships. Conflicting expectations regarding responsibilities will cause an organization to suffer.

Successful managers make expectations very clear so that their team can respond and acknowledge they understand and accept what their managers want from them. In turn, team members should be given an opportunity to outline what they expect from their management.

> "The achievements of an organization are the results of the combined effort of each individual."
>
> -- Vince Lombardi

There are several key events during an individual's employment which provide the natural opportunity for managers to set expectations. The first is at the time of hiring. Next, is during a regularly occurring performance review. The other time is when an employee is being considered for promotion. By establishing a clear understanding and commitment regarding performance expectations, managers and employees can build trust and a willingness to openly listen and speak.

If expectations are not regularly reviewed and communicated, managers can unexpectedly catch their employees off guard when conducting annual employee reviews because their expectations of performance are not aligned. This occurs all too often, and leaves managers disappointed and employees frustrated. I call this the *Surprise Theory*. An employee or team member should never be surprised during an annual or semi-annual review about an expectation their manager has of them. An employee's review and feedback about their manager should not be a surprise either.

Not setting expectations is like putting a pilot in the cockpit with no checklists or manuals and saying, "Now, fly." Setting expectations empowers employees and increases their ability to be successful in their work, which in turn provides them with greater job satisfaction. By involving them in setting the standards of acceptable performance, employees become stake-holders and can say, "I understand, and I am committed."

SETTING EXPECTATIONS: 25% - ESTABLISH EXPECTATIONS FOR MAXIMUM ACHIEVEMENT

The expectations you set as the manager must allow your team to maximize their achievement and deliver the greatest result when executed. This means that you should never set an expectation because it looks

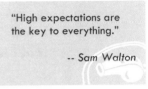

"High expectations are the key to everything."

-- Sam Walton

good on paper. Make sure it truly has the purpose to *maximize* your team's *achievement* in some capacity. When you are establishing expectations, consider the following:

- *Be exact and detailed.* Do not generalize expectations. This is not the time to be grey.

- *Be able to explain your reasoning.* We did not like it when our parents said, "Because we said so." And your team does not like it either.

- *Involve the team and be willing* to formally review, adjust, and reissue expectations on a quarterly basis.

- Develop specific result and activity based expectations. For example:
  1. At the office and ready to work by 8:00am
  2. Set five new appointments for the following week by EOB on Thursdays
  3. Conduct five follow-up appointments per week
  4. Complete and turn in your weekly report by Friday noon
  5. Achieve 110% of your quota each month

When you are setting expectations for your team, *be sure to set your own.* You want to be clear to your team on what they can expect from you, and that you will hold yourself accountable to these expectations too.

Here are some examples to consider:

> *EXAMPLE:* LEADERSHIP EXPECTATIONS
>
> 1. I will be available to my team.
> 2. I will perform 3 ride days per month with each team member.
> 3. I will inspect what I expect with each team member.

Setting clear expectations is the beginning of achieving your team's goals. A manager should give clear expectations on a regular basis throughout the year by conducting one-on-ones on a weekly, or bi-weekly, basis (*Chapter 9* covers this subject in detail). Both the manager and the employee should regularly discuss performance. Both sets of expectations should be aligned.

SETTING EXPECTATIONS: 75% - COMMUNICATION

> "The art of effective listening is essential to communication, and communication is necessary to management success."
>
> -- J. C. Penney

Inherent to most people is the desire to succeed. Therefore, if employees are not doing a good job or working on the right things, it is usually because they do not have a true understanding of expectations or the priority of expectations.

The responsibility of clearly communicating expectations resides with the manager. In order to ensure effective *communication*, a manager must write down and prioritize expectations, and then explain the reason for them.

KNOW THE STRIKE ZONE

As a sales leader, I developed a comprehensive list of expectations for all of my managers. These expectations allowed us to share a common language and understanding about how the business needed to run and what their responsibilities were to achieve team success. Some examples of my expectations included:

EXAMPLE: LEADERSHIP EXPECTATIONS

1. Lead your people and manage the business.
2. Coach and develop your team members.
3. Recognize and reward your top performers weekly.
4. Exceed sales quotas every month as a team.
5. Handle customer and employee issues immediately.
6. Do not exceed your budgeted expenses. Monitor your team's expenses.
7. Etc...

This list is only part of the expectations I set for my managers. In total, my managers had a lot of responsibilities and expectations which they had to meet. I believe as sales leaders, and sales people, we cannot guarantee results. However, *we can guarantee activity*. With such a long list of expectations, not surprisingly I would get the question, "What activities are not important?" My answer was simple, "*All* of them are important and they *all* must be completed. In order to accomplish them, you must prioritize your time."

> You cannot always guarantee results, but you can guarantee activities.

Their number one priority was developing and motivating their team members. Their next priority was implementing the coaching activities, which included team practices, one-on-ones, and street days.

For those of you who think this sounds very simple and basic, I give you my congratulations. However, the majority of companies I work with, who have similar expectations for their managers, need to improve the processes and techniques they use to train, motivate, and hold their employees accountable.

When working with my leadership consulting clients who desire improved processes, I begin by first digging into their daily activities to identify how they spend their time. Together, with the sales leader, we look at each day over the previous 30-day period. Typically, what we find is that they spent the majority of their day doing reports, attending conference calls, responding to email, and dealing with customer and employee issues. Less than 10% of their time is spent on what they felt was their number one expectation – training and motivating their employees. In business (and in life), we oftentimes get busy and consumed with daily *tasks* and forget about our most important *activities*.

CHAMPIONS AIM TOWARDS THE GOAL

Oftentimes, it is not about whether or not an employee knows what the expectations are, but more about how to prioritize them. A good example of this situation I refer to as the *Folding the Shirt Syndrome*.

Have you ever walked into a retail store and an employee is folding shirts and stocking the shelves while you wander about, hoping he might ask you if you need anything? After some minutes have passed and you realize you could benefit from his help, you eventually go to the employee. When you do finally approach him, he happily assists you although he might also just give you the finger assist (this is when he just points you in the right direction with his finger instead of actually walking you over).

Now, what you did not see is what happened 15 minutes prior to you walking in the store. Most likely the employee's boss had told him to make sure he gets the shirts folded and on the shelf before he goes on break in a few hours. So, that is *exactly* what he was focused on doing when you came into the store. This employee had no idea that he was focusing on the wrong thing.

After all, since we began school, we have been taught to focus on the *task* and not the *activity*. From the employee's perspective, he was doing the *task* the manager assigned to him. However, he has been hired as a sales clerk and the main responsibility of his *activity* should be to assist customers.

> "If you want to build a ship, don't drum up people together to collect wood and don't assign them tasks and work, but rather teach them to long for the endless immensity of the sea."
>
> -- *Antoine de Saint-Exupery*

As managers, if we *prioritize* the *expectations* we have for our employees, incidents like this retail store example would never happen. Here is an example of what the store manager could have said to his sales clerk, "O.K., while on the sales floor, you have three things you must do in the following order of priority. First, help customers even if it means stopping what you are currently doing. Second, always have a smile on your face. And third, straighten and re-stock the shelves."

I realize that perhaps this might sound very basic and one might think that most people already know these customer service skills. Sadly, this is not the case. Pay attention the next time you walk in a store. Over the next five stores you visit, see how many are doing the three expectations we just outlined to the sales clerk in our example. You will find that less than two of them will do it correctly.

Here is something even more telling. If you go to one store that does it right, and that same leader is in charge of other stores, you will find great service at all stores run by that leader. All business owners and store managers want this level of customer service, but very few achieve it. This can only be achieved by making it part of your culture and belief system, and by setting the expectations correctly at the beginning, and then holding the teams accountable.

MAKE EVERY PLAY AN OPPORTUNITY

Today, with the abundance of communication tools we possess, it is more important then ever that people not only know their expectations, but understand the priority. When you are communicating your expectations, take the time to explain *why* you have them. By doing this, you will help gain the *buy-in* necessary for successful execution.

Creating *buy-in* does not always mean that your team will agree with you. Sometimes *buy-in* is earned. The team will still need to do what is expected and may not agree with you. However as results increase, *buy-in* will be earned much like trust.

Another essential piece pertaining to expectations is accountability, which is covered in the next chapter. We will address how to achieve expectations by holding the team accountable to them.

CHAPTER 6 HIGHLIGHTS

- Setting expectations is the beginning of achieving your team's goals.

- Eliminate the *Surprise Theory* by setting expectations.

- When setting expectations for your team, be sure to set your own.

- Prioritize your team's expectations and eliminate the *Folding the Shirt Syndrome.*

- Formally re-issue expectations to each team member. Business is always changing and so will your expectations. Don't be the only one who knows when they change.

7

HOLDING YOUR TEAM ACCOUNTABLE

ac•count•able (a 'kaůn te bel) n. 1. *capable of being accounted for; explicable.*

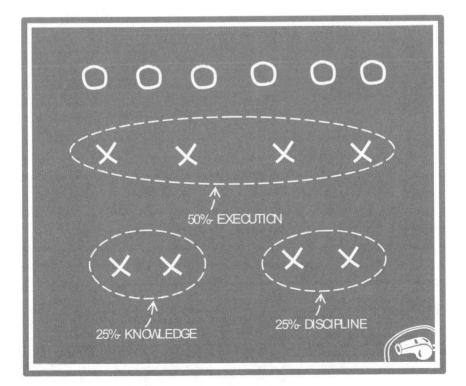

As I travel around the country and meet with different business leaders, I hear the same thing from them that I learned as a leader myself: *holding your team accountable* is a key element to building a winning team. Whether at the personal, team or organizational level, *accountability* is an essential attribute, which must be embraced and developed if you want to achieve success.

At the organizational (or team) level, *accountability* is the acknowledgement of responsibility for actions, decisions, and policies, and the obligation to report, explain and be answerable for the resulting consequences. It means *no excuses*. The willingness to be accountable for what you do and what you fail or refuse to do is crucial to success.

> "If we want unity, we must all be unifiers. If we want accountability, each of us must be accountable for all we do."
>
> -- Christine Gregoire

Unaccountable people are into excuses, blaming others, putting things off, and doing the minimum. Unaccountable people are quick to complain and slow to act. They pretend ignorance while hiding behind doors, computers, paperwork, and other people. They say things like "I didn't know," "I don't have time," "It's not my job," and "I'm just following orders." In organizations, unaccountability is a highly contagious disease.

So, if accountability is important, why do leaders oftentimes choose not to hold their teams accountable? Listed below are some of the top reasons leaders have not implemented accountability:

- They themselves do not want to be held accountable.
- They do not want to rock the boat (ostrich management; burying their head in the sand).
- They do not like or are afraid of conflict.
- They think it will take too much time.
- They do not know how.

Although accountability is important, it seems that actually implementing it is much easier said than done. In this chapter, we will focus on understanding *why* accountability is important. Then, we will focus on overcoming the barriers which might be preventing you from implementing accountability within your team. From there, you, as a leader, must develop the *want*.

ACCOUNTABILITY: 25% - KNOWLEDGE

To hold a team or person accountable is to be consistent. So let me ask you, "Do you as a leader know *why* you should hold team members accountable?"

> "Knowledge is not simply another commodity. On the contrary, knowledge is never used up. It increases by diffusion and grows by dispersion."
>
> -- Daniel J. Boorstin

Over the years, I have received many varied responses to this question. The answer in its most basic form is this: *to ensure a minimum level of production.* However, accountability should mean more than just doing the job. True accountability includes an obligation to make things better, to pursue excellence, and to do things in ways that further the goals of the organization. It is important to recognize that you do not want your team to perform purely out of fear of losing their job (although the minimum production goals might be met, exceeding them will not).

A person that performs to expectations, for the desire to win and the sense of accomplishment (*as well as* not wanting to disappoint their boss for fear of losing their job), will overachieve each and every time. Here are some simple guidelines to follow:

- Make sure that all members have a clear understanding of the expectations. You can gauge this by asking them to translate an expectation back to you. If they do not understand an expectation, how can they perform to it?

- Team members must understand the *consequences* of not meeting certain expectations.

ACCOUNTABILITY: 25% - DISCIPLINE

A successful leader must be accountable to expectations too, and should make them public to his team members. Remember, you cannot treat your team members like a parent and rely on statements like, "Do as I say, not as I do." You must stay committed to exceeding your expectations just as you want your team to exceed theirs.

Holding team members accountable takes dedication and time. A successful leader must set expectations and be willing to discipline someone who does not follow them. In order to achieve this, you must make the commitment to seek, listen, and verify in order to hold team members accountable. This requires your time.

> "The surest test of discipline is its absence."
>
> -- *Clara Barton*

Ronald Reagan is famous for saying "Trust, but verify." As a leader, you must let your team know that you trust them, but you get paid to verify. Unfortunately, since the verification process takes time, most managers opt to only trust because they rationalize they do not have the time to verify. What these managers have not learned yet is that by not taking the time to verify, everything else becomes a *waste of time*.

PAIN IS INEVITABLE – SUFFERING IS OPTIONAL

The truth is this: *having bad employees is worse than having no employees.* I once heard a manager complain, "I still have Suzie on my team because I can't find someone to replace her." In the meantime, Suzie was bringing the entire team down.

If you have someone like "Suzie" on your team, immediately move them on to "better things" (possibly out of the company). You will be amazed at how quickly your team's morale will improve – and also their performance. Having "no-body" is always better than having a "bad-body."

With the tight budget constraints of today's corporations, managers are less willing to remove a person who is not meeting expectations because they are operating under the corporate mandate that any open positions will not be filled. As a result, the managers feel they have no choice but to keep the person regardless of performance. How unfortunate that fiscal constraint is seemingly creating such a negative impact on building winning teams throughout corporations nationwide. The bottom-line is this: making a decision to keep someone who is not meeting expectations (regardless of the reason) contradicts the philosophy of holding people accountable.

> "It is time to restore the American precept that each individual is accountable for his action."
>
> -- *Ronald Reagan*

Our actions speak louder than our words when it comes to accountability. Team members will start to talk about how you say that you hold everyone accountable, but you do not really do it. They will whisper across their cubes and in the break room, "Look at Suzie! She is not meeting expectations and the manager has not done anything about her. What's the point of working hard anyway? He never fires anyone!" The *why* behind a person not being held accountable (regardless if it is a lack of employee resources or financial resources) is lost and the overarching message to the other team members is clear: "Accountability is just a theory – there is never any real action."

Imagine if a baseball team had a pitcher who walked every batter, but the owner of the team told the coach, "Hey, you can't get a new pitcher if you fire this one because we don't have the budget to replace them. But I expect you to win every game anyway!"

Sounds crazy – right? Unfortunately, this exact scenario happens in business all too often. However, there is often unseen hope in this real corporate dilemma, which I encourage you to explore. If you can identify a qualified candidate in the pipeline and are able to show corporate management the possible increase in sales and profits by making the change, then you will probably get the new hire approved.

When you take this action, you have just proven to your team your accountability to them and to your organization. True accountability means more than just doing your job. It includes an obligation to make things better, to pursue excellence, and to do things in ways that further the goals of the organization. Always be willing to rise above circumstances, to achieve the objectives of the organization. Be willing to identify problems and solve them in responsible, intelligent ways. It does not matter where the problem comes from – it might be yours or it might be inherited. The critical question is, "What are you going to do about it?"

ACCOUNTABILITY: 50% - EXECUTION

During any observation or coaching session when a team member is not meeting an expectation, you must act with assertiveness and take immediate action. When necessary, confront a situation and people in an assertive style that is straightforward without being threatening or overly aggressive. It is always best to address an issue while it is still small because if you wait it will only become bigger.

> "Effective leadership is putting first things first. Effective management is discipline in carrying it out."
>
> -- *Stephen Covey*

You have two choices in these situations. You can coach them into better performance, or you can discipline them into it. As a leader, you must decide which to use, and when. Your choice will depend upon the situation and the person. Be consistent in your decisions.

I have found that employees respect and trust the leader who holds them accountable. Although they might not always like it, they still nevertheless respect and understand accountability is imperative to the organization's success.

Discipline Is Not a Dirty Word

One of the methods I used to *inspect what I expected* and hold my team accountable involved spending a few days a week in the field. The benefit of going out in the field was two-fold. First, I was able to confirm that the sales reps were doing what they said they were doing. Second, if they were, I could spend time with the sales reps to coach them and get a better understanding of some of the obstacles they were facing on a daily basis.

On one particular occasion, one of my managers was on medical leave and had asked me if I would help inspect her team to ensure they were doing what they were supposed to be doing. It was a Saturday morning. I got in my car and drove two hours to one of her sales rep's territories. While en route, I called the sales rep and asked him what store he was training because I wanted to spend the day with him doing store visits.

After the sales rep told me which store he was at, I told him I am only ten minutes away and would meet him there. His voiced wavered and he sounded a little anxious as he replied, "Well, I am just about done at this store. Can you meet me at my next store?" I agreed and began heading towards his next store instead.

About twenty minutes later, I arrived at his next store, but he was not there. So, I called him. Knowing the reason for my call, he immediately blurted out, "I'm so sorry. I forgot that I had to stop at this other store first."

His explanation seemed reasonable enough to me. So, I told him I would just meet him there instead. I finally arrived at the third store and there he was as promised. So, we did the store visit together, and it went very well.

By the time we finished the store visit, it was already noon. So, we decided to get some lunch. While at lunch, I asked him casually what was *really* going on that morning. With his head down and his eyes diverted, he confessed: he was never at his first store. He was too embarrassed to admit it, and he decided to lie instead. Although not entirely shocked (given the way he had me driving all over the place to meet up with him), I was certainly very disappointed. After all, he was a well-paid professional, and I relied on him to be doing what he said he was doing.

We met in my office the next day to discuss the issue further. During our meeting, he agreed he had failed at his job and understood that disciplinary action was going to be taken. If we had not taken the time to inspect what we expected, then this person would have continued to not perform to his expectations. It was not long after this event that he found an opportunity outside the organization. Within a few months after a new sales rep took over sales in that territory, sales had increased by 35%.

THE QUICKER YOU GET THERE, THE SHORTER THE PAIN

Accountability goes both ways. Along with disciplinary action, we must also recognize and celebrate our team's success, even the small ones, before we expect to gain greater success. I learned this many years ago from one of the managers who reported to me.

> "Great companies have high cultures of accountability."
>
> -- Steve Ballmer

My leadership approach has always been to focus on always getting better. Due to my relentless pursuit for improvement, many people on my team felt that they could never do enough to make me happy. During a one-on-one meeting with one of my managers, she told me, "Nathan, I feel that if I don't make a touchdown I didn't do something right. What about all the *first downs*?"

Her candid remark really surprised me. I honestly thought I was recognizing her efforts, but she did not – and what she felt was what mattered. She continued, "When is it ever enough? When will you be satisfied?" After I listened to her concerns, I sat there for a minute in silence. Then, I realized – she was right. With complete conviction, I told her that I am very pleased with her and the team's performance.

I confirmed for her that 'first downs' did count, and that I would do a better job in celebrating even the smallest victories.

From that day forward, I made it one of my expectations for myself to take time daily and weekly to recognize my team's small victories. The lesson she taught me made me a better leader. Up until that meeting, I had *only* focused on the belief that we would never be satisfied nor would we ever stop focusing on getting better. However, along the way, I needed to tell my team just how proud I was of them of every success we achieved. I learned to be sure to recognize the small accomplishments on the way to the big ones and make it public.

In summary, pay attention to the baby steps people take along the way as they strive to reach the ultimate goals set by management. Encourage them along the path by showing appreciation for what has been accomplished along the way.

CHAPTER 7 HIGHLIGHTS

- Accountability is the key to building a winning team.

- A person that performs to expectations for the desire to win and for a sense of accomplishment as well as not wanting to disappoint their leader versus the fear of losing their job will overachieve every time.

- "Trust, but verify". - Ronald Reagan

- By retaining someone that is not meeting expectations for any reason regardless of limited employee resources or limited financial resources contradicts the practice of holding people accountable.

- Hold yourself accountable to celebrate the small victories on the way to achieve the big victories.

8

DEVELOPING A
BUSINESS PLAN

plan ('plan) n. 1. *a way of procedure; a method of action.*

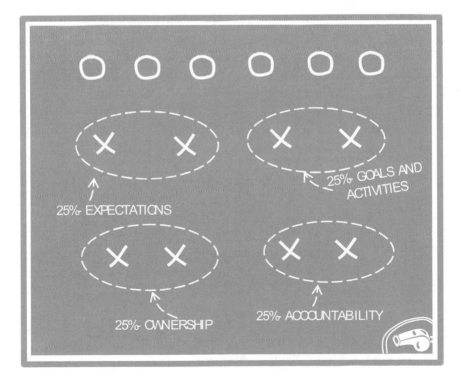

Would you trust a general who went to war without a plan? Would you admire a coach who sent his team onto the field without a game plan? How about a builder – would you allow them to build your house without a plan? The answer to these questions is obvious – no.

Let us take a moment and consider a business plan. Should a bank consider loaning money to a company without a plan? Bankers would undoubtedly answer, "No." Given the importance of having a plan, I believe it would it be safe to conclude that having a plan is important.

Many companies talk about having plans and the importance of them. I remember when I was working for a large company where sometimes the vice presidents received their plans half-way through the fiscal year. By the time these plans got to the front-line troops, the year end was less than 90 days away.

Can you imagine a football coach giving the players his game plan *after* the kick-off?

One of the reasons why delays occur while developing and communicating a business plan is the constant change of goals, budgets, and focus points. This causes many companies to delay communicating their overall plan. Most large companies have at one point or another experienced this problem, but they are certainly not alone. These delays can often plague smaller companies who have a limited number of resources to get the work done.

It is not uncommon for individuals and organizations to struggle with creating a business plan. My clients frequently tell me that they have a plan in their head. In response to this, I inform them that having a plan in their head is not the same as having a business plan – it is called having a thought. Before an organization can maximize their results, they must have a plan. And although creating the business plan is only the beginning, we cannot start without one.

The purpose behind developing a business plan is to turn thoughts and ideas into intentional behaviors and actions. Once a plan is in place, we can track our results. Periodically, business plans should be reviewed and adjustments made to ensure it remains current based on changes to the business environment.

A business plan must be reviewed and adjusted often.

With a solid business plan in place, the real work and the greatest results begin to take focus. These results are determined by the plans the frontline employees create and the adjustments made to their plans on a monthly and quarterly basis.

HE WHO RUNS IN CIRCLES NEVER GETS ANYWHERE

Of the companies that actually develop business plans, they usually draft a plan once a year, but will not review it again until it is time to update it a year later. This tactic is a *sure plan to fail!* Just like game plans for sports team and war plans for the military, business plans must be constantly adjusted to reflect new developments in the field. A business plan should be a living document with coffee stains and tattered edges. If your business plan is sitting nicely bound on the shelf with a thick layer of dust, your business could be at risk. If your business plan is just sitting on your bookshelf, or stashed away in a drawer, it is just as useful as your entire collection of half-read improvement books. A business plan should be reviewed frequently if not daily and adjusted as necessary not just annually.

Of all the plays covered in this book, I have found that most people and organizations struggle with reviewing and updating their business plan the most. Many times it seems that we just cannot find time in our week, or year for that matter, to make adjustments to our plan. Instead, we make adjustments in our activity as we go. The following plays will cover the *why* of creating your business plan as well as the *how* to update it and make adjustments to it on a regular basis. Most importantly, creating a business plan provides you a tool to use when developing your team members and holding them accountable to meeting and exceeding your expectations.

DEVELOPING A PLAN: 25% - EXPECTATIONS

Although expectations were covered at length in a previous play, they are a necessary component to developing a business plan. Setting expectations is important to building trust and respect with your employees, customers, business partners, and suppliers. Each one of these constituents is vitally important to your business. They need to know exactly what is expected of them.

> "If you accept the expectations of others, especially negative ones, then you never will change the outcome."
>
> -- Michael Jordan

Communication is important to disseminating expectations to your constituents. A business plan provides the ideal vehicle by which your expectations can be communicated. Once you have started your business, you will need to continue making expectations.

All constituents involved with your company need to know what is expected of them and expected of your company. Employees, in particular, need to know exactly what is expected of them to get the job done. By knowing the goals of the company and organization, they can correlate the results and outcome of their labor. They also need to know what has to be done to receive a promotion and to excel in their work.

DEVELOPING A PLAN: 25% - GOALS AND ACTIVITIES

Employees are always looking to better themselves through their work. They are looking for promotions, rewards, and education. In order to achieve this, they need clear expectations set so they can realize their potential as employees and human beings living and working for their livelihood. Excellent performance must be defined to the employee.

The way to do this is to review the business plan with your team and have each team member develop their own business plan based on the expectations outlined in the overall plan. Once expectations have been developed, specific goals and specific activities (other than what was provided in the company business plan) should be developed to assist each team member in accomplishing his set goals.

As a leader, I would provide the following instruction to my managers and sales people when they were developing their business plans:

- All employees need to develop a business plan including my support staff. I want everybody to have a stake in the game and a personal plan on how they are going to win their part.

- Each person has to use my expectations given to them as the minimum, and create a plan that will exceed the minimums.

- Everyone must stretch themselves and achieve things beyond those accomplished in the past.

- The plans need to be very specific on what, when, and how they plan on doing activities.

- Each team member must show how they will exceed these expectations, and what they will use to measure their success.

- Each team member has to be ready to present their business plan to their peers and their superiors on a quarterly basis – this will make it public. The group will see what each person is doing and work together to hold each other accountable.

Once the team developed and presented their business plans, I scheduled regular meetings to review the details and overall goals of the plans. During the meeting, we would discuss the strengths and weaknesses of the plan. Team members were encouraged to share ideas and ask questions. From these meetings, adjustments would be made to keep the plans aligned with the overall goals of the company and our team.

> "Every minute you spend in your life is either spent bringing you closer to your goals or moving you away from your goals."
>
> -- *Bo Bennett*

The goals and activities set by each team member provided personal motivation to be part of the process in creating value for the company and customers. They felt valued; therefore, they could create value.

DEVELOPING A PLAN: 25% - OWNERSHIP

In order to achieve the goals of your company and organization, you must involve your team. Your employees are the lifeblood of your company – without them you will not succeed. Remember one of the never waiving expectations in your plan is that you will be successful!

If as a leader you hand your team the entire *playbook*, you might assure that the team will *follow* it, but they will not likely *exceed* it. By having your team participate in developing the *playbook*, your team gains ownership of the plan to achieve the given goals. With plans in place, follow up with regular update meetings. Keep the team informed of all changes in the overall plan and goals. This will prevent team members from following an old goal that no longer applies.

> "Plans are nothing. Planning is everything."
>
> -- Dwight D. Eisenhower

With a personal plan in place, team members can then supervise themselves in terms of the plan. If the plan is set-up properly, your team will do whatever is necessary to accomplish the desired results within the guidelines. As their leader, you can serve as a source for help and advice instead of overseeing their daily activities.

DEVELOPING A PLAN: 25% - ACCOUNTABILITY

When you ask your team to present their business plans publicly to an audience of peers and management, you are assuring that they will not only want to hold themselves accountable to it (*"I said I would do something in front of everyone, I better do it!"*), but you are assuring that their peers and management team will help too (*"Hey, you said you would do this – now do it!"*).

I recommend you use the following criteria when reviewing the business plans presented by your team:

- Criteria 1: Did you do what you said you were going to do?

- Criteria 2: What are you going to do next quarter?

If you decide to implement this process within your organization, it is imperative that you stay committed and consistent with your quarterly review sessions.

CRITERIA 1: DID YOU DO IT?

It was the third week of March. All of the managers were scheduled to present their first quarter results and share their second quarter business plan with their peers and me. During the first week in March, I, as their leader, had already presented to them my business plan for the second quarter to ensure they had plenty of time to make changes on their business plans based on any and all new information or expectations I had for them.

> "Desire is the key to motivation, but it's determination and commitment to an unrelenting pursuit of your goal that will enable you to attain the success you seek."
>
> -- *Mario Andretti*

Each manager was given one hour to present their previous quarter's performance. Copies of their previous quarter's plans were copied and distributed. This gave each manager the opportunity to compare what the manager had presented three months ago versus what their actual results showed. This review process was an essential tool I used to hold them accountable to not just me, but to their peers.

Each manager was asked to present the following performance data:

- Monthly budget and team goals versus actual results

- Committed activities versus what actually got done

- What worked and what did not work

- Three greatest struggles and three best practices

Interestingly enough, the most interactive discussions took place when the topic moved to their greatest struggles and best practices. As a team, each manager would help out another

> "The object of all work is accomplishment and there must be planning intelligence, and honest purpose, as well as perspiration. Seeming to do is not doing."
>
> -- Thomas A. Edison

with obstacles by sharing what he might have done when he experienced the same or similar obstacle. By working together as a team, we were able to solve the problems for each other.

My personal favorite was when the managers shared best practices. During the first few reviews, I noticed the managers would often hold back one or two things (as if they did not want to give up their *top secrets*). However, after a few meetings, and experiencing firsthand how giving up their best practices actually allowed them to gain more, they joined in with enthusiasm. After all, each time they gave away one *top secret* they gained nine in return (one from each manager who was holding back too). During this time, they could be a star. They shared what they felt contributed to their success – success they had earned by planning diligently and working even harder.

CRITERIA 2: WHAT ABOUT NEXT QUARTER?

After we finished reviewing the manager's previous quarter, it was time for them to share their commitments of what their team was going to deliver next quarter. The goal of this activity was not to create extra work for my managers, or to re-write an entire business plan. The main purpose was to make slight adjustments, and course corrections, in order to improve results and maximize sales potential in the upcoming quarter.

Each manager was given about 45 minutes to present their projected performance for the upcoming quarter. Copies of the plan were distributed. They started by presenting what sales they would commit to versus their actual budget. This topic always made for great discussion. Next (and the part I always considered the most interesting), they presented the activities they were going to do and hold their team accountable to do on a daily, weekly and monthly basis. This would then become the new measurement tool we would use during our one-on-one meetings as well as become what I would hold them accountable to execute over the next three months.

KEEP THE BALL IN PLAY

I have seen many leaders try to implement this program only to let it dwindle down to a once a year, or a *'When We Can'* exercise. I guarantee that this half-hearted effort will not generate the results you are seeking. In fact, I attribute much of my leadership success to implementing this *exact* program.

This program works if you diligently work it; not only did it hold my team accountable, it held me accountable to my team. To obtain the desired results, it required my involvement as a team coach. I also had to regularly share information with them so that they could meet their commitments to me and each other.

> "Obstacles don't have to stop you. If you run into a wall, don't turn around and give up. Figure out how to climb it, go through it, or work around it."
>
> -- Michael Jordan

In one organization where I worked, we took the program a step further. Beginning with my leader, he held his meeting with us on the last week of the second month of each quarter. Then, I conducted my meeting with my managers on the third week of the last month in the quarter. Lastly, my managers held their meetings with their employees on the first week of the first month in the new quarter. Diagramed below is an example of a *Quarterly Review Calendar*:

EXAMPLE: SECOND QUARTER REVIEW CALENDAR

1. Vice Presidents Quarterly Review   2/28/2007
2. Directors Quarterly Review   3/21/2007
3. Managers Quarterly Review   4/01/2007

These presentations, when done regularly, become instrumental in holding each team member accountable. As a side benefit, it also gave each person an opportunity to practice presenting to a group thus working on their presentation skills – another important sales skill!

KEEP YOUR EYE ON THE PRIZE

Developing personal business plans for each team member is all about getting desired results. As their leader, your basic attitude should be one of "Where do you want to go?" or "What are your goals, and how can I help you?" Then downstream the resulting attitude becomes, "How is it going, and what can I do to help?"

Next, allow each team member to evaluate themselves. Since they have a clear understanding of what results are expected and what criteria are used to assess their performance, they are in a great position to evaluate themselves. Involving your team in establishing the business plan and evaluating their performance builds a high level of trust. The higher their trust is of the process the more accurate, more complete, and more honest their evaluation will be of themselves (more than your evaluation could ever be). After all, they know all the details.

Whatever we believe about our team becomes self-fulfilling – at least, we will produce the evidence to support our view. So, trust them to do the right thing by giving them the room to succeed based on their own fuel with regular maintenance provided by you.

CHAPTER 8 HIGHLIGHTS

- Although creating a business plan is only the beginning, we cannot start without one.

- Having a plan in your head is not a plan – it is just a thought.

- A business plan should be a living document with coffee stains and tattered edges – not nicely bound on the bookshelf covered in twelve-month-old dust.

- By asking each team member to develop their specific goals and activities in their business plan, it ensures they will own their goals and activities.

- The quarterly review presentations help hold all team members accountable and allow each team member to practice and improve their presentation skills.

9

ONE-ON-ONE COACHING SESSIONS

coach•ing ('koch ing) v. *1. to impart, as knowledge before unknown, or rules for practice; to train by special instruction; to direct.*

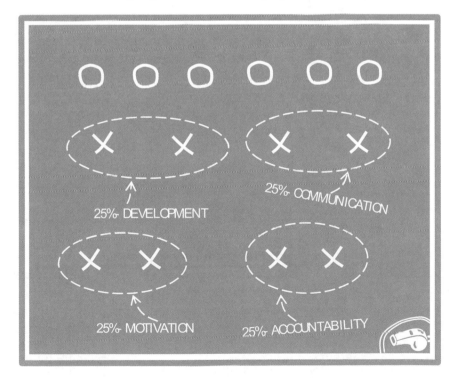

One-on-one coaching sessions are a key activity that leaders should provide to their team. These sessions go well beyond giving straightforward instruction. They involve more than just sitting down with an employee for 30 to 45 minutes shooting the breeze or giving updates. It is a structured coaching activity intended to deliver clear insights and specific results.

While they should address task outcomes and how to achieve them, this time should also be spent addressing attitudes, discipline, morale, ethics, and career development. In short, one-on-ones provide the ideal setting to achieve the following objectives:

- Communicate individually without interruptions

- Identify knowledge, skills, and abilities requiring development

- Hold individuals accountable by reviewing expectations

- Motivate individuals by recognizing success

One-on-one coaching sessions provide a setting that is without interruptions and distractions. As a leader, one-on-ones help you stay aware of your team's activities and focus. It is the ideal time to review an individual's progress and provide feedback on achieving goals as set forth in a business plan. Lastly, one-on-ones are a great time to give well deserved praise. However, do not give insincere praise – never use praise as 'filler' when an employee does not deserve it.

> "The only thing worse than a coach or CEO who doesn't care about his people is one who pretends to care. People can spot a phony every time."
>
> -- Jimmy Johnson

In fact, you will find, after conducting one-on-ones with your team members for a period of time, your team will come to anticipate them with enthusiasm. They will appreciate your coaching and the time you spend with them. One-on-ones show the members of your team that you care about them and that they are valued enough to receive your time, attention, and coaching.

THE AIR OFFERS LESS RESISTANCE THAN DIRT

By this point, I do hope you recognize the importance of one-on-one coaching sessions. However, I realize that some of you still need to break down a few more barriers before you are willing to believe. In this section, I will cover some common myths, which have held back some managers from adopting this leadership technique.

Myth 1: "I don't need to have one-on-ones with my employees. After all, I talk to them everyday."

During my initial interactions with most managers, the most common remark made by them prior to implementing one-on-one coaching sessions is something like this, "Why should I have one-on-ones with my employees? I talk or see them every day. By the way, I also have an open door policy; so, my employees can come see me any time they need me. This technique is for other managers that don't communicate with their teams on a regular basis – not me."

One-on-one coaching sessions do not replace daily communication – they, in fact, are completely different. During our daily conversations and interactions, how often do we actually stop to discuss the activities of our employees, or role-play telemarketing or sales calls? And although most managers have an open door policy, most sales people do not actually walk into their manager's office every week and say, "Hey, Boss. I am sure glad you have an open door policy. Can we spend the next 30 minutes role-playing a sales call?"

The reality is this: every team can benefit from implementing one-on-one coaching sessions. Besides, what bad thing could happen from setting aside scheduled time with every member on your team?

Myth 2: "I just don't have the time to do it."

Perhaps you are a business owner or manager who thinks you are too busy with your own work to spend extra time training or boosting employee morale. Although you are busy and have a lot of responsibilities, consider this: your leadership and coaching *helps create* motivated, productive employees. In turn, these high-performance employees will lighten your workload. The real question to answer is, "Can you afford not to?"

One-on-one sessions along with other formal and informal employee development tools, such as monthly, quarterly or annual performance appraisals do work and are used by highly successful companies to bring out the best in their employees.

PRE-GAME CHECKLIST

Now, that you are completely onboard (or at least willing to consider) one-on-one coaching sessions, I am going to walk through a checklist designed to help you prepare for your meetings – much like a checklist pilots use before every take off.

Your one-on-one checklist consists of four main components – each containing detailed actions designed to aid your preparation for your one-on-ones:

- Communication
- Accountability
- Development
- Motivation

Even after you become comfortable and confident in conducting your one-on-one coaching sessions, I encourage you to continue using this checklist. Although I am certain all pilots with extensive flying experience know everything on the checklist, they continue to use it to ensure they do not miss anything because hundreds of passengers are counting on them to safely fly the plane. Remember, as the leader, your team members are counting on you to help them grow and succeed for themselves and to provide for their families.

ONE-ON-ONES: 25% - COMMUNICATION

Communication between managers and employees is an important part of any organization. Employees want guidelines from you as their leader, and you want input from your entire team. When one-on-ones are conducted on a regular basis and in a structured manner, they are a great communication tool.

They are also a good way for a leader to stay connected with what is going on within the organization. Although most companies have little trouble communicating downward, they typically struggle to get information to flow upward. When employees stay quiet about what they need, the negative results can include missed opportunities, delayed projects, and failed initiatives.

The key to getting your team to communicate better and to keeping their progress on track is to build a quality interaction between you and your team. It takes a concerted, ongoing effort to keep the channels of communication open and active, but the payoff is immeasurable. One-on-one coaching sessions provide the ideal forum to encourage employees to communicate with you, advance strategic vision, and attain goals.

ONE-ON-ONES: 25% - ACCOUNTABILITY

One-on-ones are designed to hold our team members accountable to exceed expectations. However, as leaders, we too must hold ourselves accountable to conducting them on a regular basis. Most managers decide they want to implement this program because they know it will help them. Yet, it does not always happen because they do not hold themselves accountable to making it work.

> "Your expectation opens or closes the doors of your supply. If you expect grand things, and work honestly for them, they will come to you, your supply will correspond with your expectation."
>
> -- Orison Swett Marden

Make the Time

The hardest part of planning one-on-ones is scheduling the time to make it happen (time can be the root of all problems). Remember, regardless of how little time you have, you must find the time. Sometimes, the only way to *find* the time is by *taking* the time. Be creative – look for a time early in the morning, late in the day, after street days, etc. When you do come up with a time, put it on your calendar and treat it as if it is the biggest prospect you have.

Keep in mind that your schedule might vary depending on the number of people directly reporting to you. Ideally, having weekly one-on-ones with each team member is best, but, if you have a large number of direct reports, every other week is workable.

It is very easy for managers to get busy managing the business, attending meetings and conference calls, writing and responding to emails, dealing with HR issues, and doing management reports. More times than not, this can keep us from doing what is the most important part of our job, which is coaching and developing our team members. To overcome these time barriers and gain buy-in, you may want to meet with your manager. When you show your manager your plan to increase productivity and sales by prioritizing your schedule with coaching one-on-ones and team practices, you *will* get his support and commitment.

> "Outstanding leaders go out of their way to boost the self-esteem of their personnel. If people believe in themselves, it's amazing what they can accomplish."
>
> -- *Sam Walton*

Notify Your Team

As part of your expectations, you need to have set times for your one-on-ones and notify your team members. They may be specific days and even down to specific times. Never surprise your team members with a structured one-on-one. Put the one-on-ones on your calendar and be sure your team does the same (this does not mean you cannot pull a team member aside anytime for ad-hoc updates or reviews).

Your one-on-ones should not to replace the every day communication that you have with your team members.

There should be no surprises, your team members should know what you plan to cover. Preparation should *not* include having your team member prepare a report to review with you – this activity would take away from his or her selling or productivity. Instead, you need to be sure you are using the current business plan and any reports that are already in place.

ONE-ON-ONES: 25% - DEVELOPMENT

If you have conducted a street day with a team member recently, or attended a training session, have your notes and information available. This way you can discuss areas they can improve on as well as reiterate and recognize their success. You will find your agenda will not change dramatically from meeting to meeting, so there is no reason why you should be unable to prepare one.

DEVELOP AN AGENDA

You are best qualified to determine what agenda items fit your team, but make sure the agenda items in your one-on-ones are meaningful and productive. Do not have fluff items. Have your team member's business plan in hand, an outline of the items to cover, and specific examples of what your team member did. Be prepared. Do not wing one-on-ones. Believe me – your team will know.

A common mistake managers often make after conducting several one-on-ones is that they eliminate the agenda. They rationalize that since the session is always the same, why create one. If you catch yourself beginning to think like that, I encourage you to remember that the agenda is there to keep you *on track* and *focused*.

Listed on the next page, are two sample one-on-one coaching agendas for you to use as the basis for developing your own custom agendas.

ONE-ON-ONE AGENDA
WITH A BUSINESS TO BUSINESS SALES EXECUTIVE

- Review weekly pipeline, pending sales, and last week's results.

- Go over previous and current week's scheduled appointments.

- Set 3 activity goals for the week and review the previous week's goals.

- Discuss any major prospect or customers and identify an action plan to help them.

- Work on sales skills development.

- Role-play a sales call or prospecting call to practice.

ONE-ON-ONE AGENDA
WITH A SALES MANAGER

- Review current sales and pending sales.

- Discuss each person on their team and their status.

- Review any possible new candidates and check status of the bench of perspective new sales reps.

- Review their business plan and activity status.

- Set 3 goals for the week and review last week's goals.

- Develop next week's training topic for their team.

ONE-ON-ONES: 25% - MOTIVATION

An effective coach is one who shows workers how to get the job done; keeps them informed, helps individuals experiencing job (or company) related problems, listens *(really listens)* to employees, gives credit and praise when it is due, and always directs negative feedback at performance and results – never people.

> "To get at their real concerns, there is simply no substitute for talking one-on-one."
>
> -- *Sonny Perdue*

One of the concepts many new managers are taught (and many veteran managers do on a regular basis because they were taught to do it) is to preface negative feedback with something positive. I do not subscribe to that theory because I believe it tarnishes the coaching aspect of the job and creates the wrong environment. Unfortunately, this approach is misused all the time. Many managers will say, "You did this item very well, BUT you need to improve on this item." In other instances, the manager will use an insincere compliment to soften the blow of the constructive feedback thus causing more damage than good.

My personal theory to improvement is as follows: I want to improve, and, in order to improve, I must be helped to notice when I need improvement. As a leader, I would tell my managers, "In order for you to get to the next level, we need to work on _____ *(a particular part)* of your leadership. Here is what I have observed is not working as well as you are intending it to work." By structuring my conversation this way, I remain genuine in my coaching without appearing insulting or demeaning.

My interest remains focused on making my people better every day – not making them feel better by coddling them. In short, only give positive feedback that is truly positive feedback, and use constructive feedback to explain and teach how to get better.

REMINDERS AND FINAL THOUGHTS

The keys for maximum one-on-one coaching session results are:

- Always conduct them in a office without distractions

- Be consistent

- Have an agenda

- Stay on point

- Make it a priority

- Keep it to a maximum of one hour

Coaching is a process – not a one shot deal. Successful coaching sessions with employees take time to develop – be patient. The risk of trying something new is definitely worth the potential profit.

CHAPTER 9 HIGHLIGHTS

- One-on-one coaching sessions are one of the key coaching activities a leader can do for their team members.

- Stay committed and consistent by having an agenda and a scheduled date and time for every coaching session.

- Do not create extra reports or work for the employee or yourself for your coaching sessions. Use whatever reports, business plans or calendar documents that you and your sales team regularly uses to conduct business.

- One-on-ones are designed and implemented to hold teams accountable to exceed expectations while holding the leader accountable to coaching and developing his or her team.

- Have each team member develop specific, personal goals, and activities in a business plan to ensure he or she owns them.

10

EFFECTIVE SALES MEETINGS

ef•fec•tive (i 'fek tiv) adj. 1. *producing a decided, decisive, or desired result; impressive, striking.*

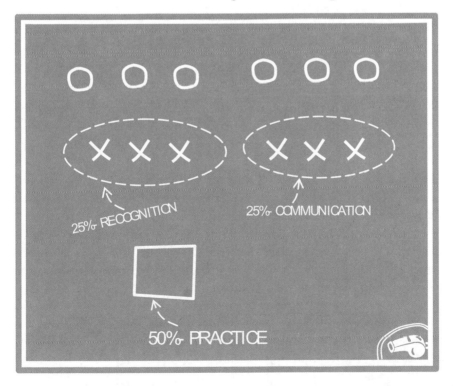

Have you ever said or thought, "Sales meetings are a waste of time." When one of my sales managers would tell me that their sales people felt their sales meetings were a waste of their time, I knew I had a management issue. The really scary part is that this is a very common statement made by most sales people (and even sales managers) in most companies. However, this remark does not stem from a problem with the sales person or manager making the statement. Instead, it stems from a problem with the organizational set-up and expectations of the sales managers.

If you, your team, or organization wonders why you have sales meetings, then it is time for a change. To begin, stop having sales meetings to review what is happening, what is not happening, and giving out new company changes. Instead, start conducting weekly sales *practices*. This does not mean that there will not be small informational items communicated, but the focus should be on *teaching* your team – not reviewing what is already obvious. If you start treating your sales team like a professional sports team (by *practicing* and *training*), you will start winning championships!

TURN SALES MEETINGS INTO TEAM PRACTICE MEETINGS

It was in 1995 when I first witnessed a manager turning our sales meetings into sales practice meetings. The manager was Adam Hochfelder, and he had been recently promoted to sales manager.

Before the promotion, Adam had been my peer for the past two years. We had joined the company around the same time. During our two years of working together, we had both focused on getting better at our jobs as sales people, and took training into our own hands. We began by cold-calling each other from our office phones to practice our telemarketing skills. Then, we began spending time before or after work role-playing sales appointments.

When he got promoted and became my boss, I was excited for him while also feeling concerned about how he would be as a leader for the team. I did not question his knowledge or skill, but because I viewed him as my peer I did not know how he would be as my manager. However, Adam left no time to question his promotion and immediately began making a difference.

At our first sales meeting, Adam announced we were going to start conducting our sales meetings differently. Our sales meetings would become team sales *practice* meetings. He asked for each person to give skill topics for us to practice during our meetings. Each person was given a topic: telemarketing, cold-calling, in-person sales calls, asking qualifying questions, closing the sale, etc. Our sales practice meetings began with our very first meeting, and every meeting thereafter we would spend time training or practicing as a team.

Our sales meetings were no longer a painful event of getting new information from our boss and reviewing sales updates followed by the group dwelling on the negatives. There now was a way for us to practice and get better.

PERFECTING THE PRACTICE

In 1996, I was promoted to the Sales Manager for the New Orleans market with a large company. I took what Adam started in 1995 and enhanced it over the next twelve years. Since that time, I have implemented a similar program in numerous sales teams across the country. I found that, when I replaced sales meetings with sales practice meetings, the results of my teams exponentially increased.

> "Don't do anything in practice that you wouldn't do in the game."
>
> -- George Halas

In each meeting, we would have three components: *recognition*, *communication*, and *practice*. I always use the word *practice* versus *training* because it was not about learning a new skill or product. Instead, it was about practicing and improving on the basic skills.

SALES MEETINGS: 25% - RECOGNITION

Most employees do not do work for salary alone (really, this is true – believe it or not). They want and need *recognition*. And it is not a new desire of people; we have been striving for recognition since we were children. Back then, we wanted it from our parents and teachers. If we did well on a test or report card, we would wait for our parents to tell us how proud they were of us. We would mow the lawn or clean the kitchen without being asked (rarely, but we did) just to hear our parents thank us and recognize our work (and perhaps a small part of us wanted to be paid too). Like most things in life we did not outgrow our need for recognition. It just evolved and shifted to seeking recognition from our employers and peers.

A top complaint of employees about their employer is feeling underappreciated and not recognized enough for their efforts. But the solution for this is not to go up to your employees and start praising them. If you recognize everybody on a regular basis for basic achievements, it will diminish the recognition for outstanding ones.

Recognition must be earned. The key is to recognize the top performers – those that went above and beyond. Recognition should be a part of your weekly practice, but it should not stop there. Be certain to recognize achievement at every opportunity available. Just make sure it is valid recognition.

THE KINGPIN AWARD

Weekly sales practice meetings are a great time to recognize the best performer in some special way. This does not need to be a monetary reward costing the company. Consider developing a *traveling trophy* instead. It can be handed from the previous week's winner to the current week's winner.

As a sales director, one of my favorite recognition pieces was a *Kingpin of the Week* award. It was an actual bowling pin. To acquire it, I went to the local bowling alley and told them why I needed a bowling pin. And the owners were very happy to donate it to my team. Every week the top manager was awarded the *Kingpin of the Week* award based on certain performance criteria.

> "If it doesn't matter who wins or loses, then why do they keep score?"
>
> -- Vince Lombardi

Amazingly enough, the managers *fought* over the bowling pin and *loved* tugging it out of each others' hand. Bottom line, the award which cost the company *nothing* ended up meaning *everything* to my management team. This system for reward eventually was passed down to every sales team in our organization. Many managers used a fishing pole and called it the *Catch of the Week* award. Another manager used a baseball bat calling it the *Homerun of the Week* award.

INTERNAL COMPETITION IS HEALTHY

There are some people in business who believe internal competition is unhealthy. I disagree 100% - I believe internal competition is a great way to motivate and recognize. Having said this, it is essential that the competition be conducted in a healthy manner. Internal competition needs to be fun and used as a tool to recognize those who are achieving great things.

> "People who are unable to motivate themselves must be content with mediocrity."
>
> -- Andrew Carnegie

Not everybody in an organization is going to necessarily like the competition. However, just like with many things in life, you cannot please everybody. Interestingly enough, across the board, I have discovered that the people who fit the attribute and skill sets I look for when hiring for my sales teams *like* the competition.

The reality of internal competition is this: unless an organization uses a flat raise system giving everyone the same pay increase every year, or promotes by tenure only, we compete every day for our raise percentage or the next promotion. As for me, I will hire the willing competitor who wants to win the game every time over the complacent person.

SALES MEETINGS: 25% - COMMUNICATION

Although weekly sales practices should focus on practicing, the fact of corporate life is that there are updates and information that needs to be shared. We all want to be informed about new things going on within the organization and plans for the future, so share it with the team. The key is to share the required information and move on. Do not make the majority of your meeting about updates.

With technology today, most information is sent out immediately through email or text messaging. A good rule of thumb is to have a set amount of time to give or review any information that needs to be shared with the team. Be sure to allow enough time for each person to get up and share where they are as well. Once again, this brings ownership to their results. This can be very effective if managed correctly. This is not a time to complain or start a complaint session.

In my meetings, I was very conscious of the energy and the tone of each meeting. I wanted it to be positive, while being effective. We could discuss obstacles and issues as long as it was to find a solution and not to create a negative morale.

SALES MEETINGS: 50% - PRACTICE

At this point, you might be wondering, "Should we start calling our sales meetings sales practice meetings from now on?" The simple answer is: YES. Let me share with you how we took what Adam started in 1995 and continued to build and grow it. Much like everything we have talked about, we never stopped improving our coaching program.

I was meeting with a sales manager who had been with the company for several years. We were discussing things that we could do to help his team increase sales. I asked him about his sales meetings. He told me that he held them twice a month to make his previous manager happy, but he honestly felt they were a waste of time.

At this point, I mentioned to him that, when you have effective sales meetings, which allow people to practice their skills, you always get value from the meeting. Then, it is not a *waste of time*. We discussed how he conducted his meetings, and he told me what topics and information they discussed during their meetings. We decided it would be good for me to observe his next meeting in order to experience it firsthand.

His meeting was similar to 'typical sales meetings' I had seen in the past. There was an agenda and time was spent going over previous sales, obstacles, company updates, and the following week's goals. Then, it ended. At the completion of the meeting, I agreed with the manager that it was a waste of the sales people's time too. After all, they did not *learn* anything or *practice*.

> "Restlessness is discontent – and discontent is the first necessity of progress. Show me a thoroughly satisfied man – and I will show you a failure."
>
> -- *Thomas A. Edison*

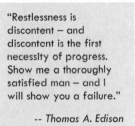

After the meeting, the manager and I sat down, and I explained the vision of building a number one team. I told him that to be the best we must stop *managing* the team and start *coaching* our sales people. I also told him that a key part of any team (or person) getting better at a skill is to *practice*. I used a golfing analogy (since this manager golfed) to paint a clear picture stating, "The more you practice your golf swing the better you get at the game." Then I asked him a very simple question, "Since you get paid to lead a sales team, when was the last time you practiced selling with your team?" There was dead silence.

He never did answer. Instead, we immediately began creating a training program for him and his team. We first agreed that he would train and coach every sales person on a *daily* basis in addition to conducting weekly sales practice meetings. It became his job to really focus on his team's comprehension of new and continuous programs.

This manager (and soon thereafter all managers within my department) was now focused on conducting weekly *sales practice meetings* – not sales meetings. This was not just a *title change*. It was a *focus change*.

During their *sales practice meetings*, they spent time recognizing the top performer and discussing company updates and promotions still, but then spent the *majority* of the time learning a sales lesson and role – playing (practicing). The meetings were no longer a waste of time because the team was learning and practicing. And most importantly, they were focused on getting better.

THEY WERE MORE MOTIVATED

After a few months, the manager and I sat down to review how the new and improved sales *practice* meetings were impacting his team. He stated with enthusiasm that they have seen an improvement in sales and more importantly in his team's skills. Everyone (both the strong sales people and the weaker ones) were improving their basic skills of prospecting and conducting more effective sales calls. But one thing he said, which he did not expect, was that his team members were more motivated to prospect and go on sales calls.

Let us break down what motivation is. This is the hidden golden nugget in my opinion. When a person practices, they become more knowledgeable by developing a new skill or improving on an existing one. By obtaining greater knowledge, they feel more confident in themselves. With an increase in their confidence of their abilities, they become more motivated to take action. This formula could be broken down to look like this:

PRACTICE = KNOWLEDGE = CONFIDENCE = MOTIVATION

In turn, the resulting increase in motivation spurs more practice thus producing more knowledge, greater confidence, and even more motivation. Once the cycle is completed successfully, it becomes self-sustaining by the individual's drive to improve.

The manager in this story is not alone. I find more sales teams not practicing on a regular basis than those that do. Ask yourself and your team, "Are your sales meetings a waste of time?"

PRACTICE PUTS BRAINS ON YOUR MUSCLES

For a moment, think about your weekly sales practice meetings as weekly *motivational events* and how that would affect your team. How many times have you gone to see a motivational speaker and left feeling pumped up? You have a whole new list of activities and goals you are going to implement. Although, on occasion it looks very similar to the list you created when you saw the previous motivational speaker a year prior. Nonetheless, you leave ready to get things done. But a few weeks later you are right back to where you were. The motivation wore off.

> "Always bear in mind that your own resolution to succeed is more important than any other one thing."
>
> -- Abraham Lincoln

What happened? Is it that the motivation did not work? No – this is not true. Instead, let us look at what did occur. Motivation should be perceived as a form of *energy*. Science has revealed that as humans we are made up of energy. So, what if we ate a huge dinner one night and then did not eat for a week? The answer is simple: we would become hungry. But would we argue that the food we ate did not work? No.

Instead of getting motivated once a year, your team should get motivated weekly, thus staying fueled and energized on a weekly basis. Bottom line, it is up to you as the leader to make sure sales meetings are not a waste of time. Instead, position them so that they become the cornerstone of making a winning sales team.

GET IN FORMATION

Now that we have explored the advantages and benefits of weekly *sales practice meetings*, it is time for you to put it into action for you and your team. Be patient and give your team (and yourself) time to become acclimated to this new approach. As with any change, there will be people who embrace it and others that grumble and complain. Given some time, the new meeting structure will become easy to follow and the benefits will pay off.

To further aid you in kicking off this new sales meeting approach, I have provided a sample agenda for a weekly *Sales Practice Meeting*, which is listed below. Use it to guide you in the development of your own agenda.

TELE-PROSPECTING TEAM PRACTICE SCHEDULE	
8:00 AM	"Traveling Trophy" Weekly Sales Recognition for the Top Rep
8:10 AM	Tele-prospecting training (*How to effectively tele-market to target clients*)
8:50 AM	Company and Team Updates
9:05 AM	Round Table Discussion
9:15 AM	Meeting Adjourned

CHAPTER 10 HIGHLIGHTS

- Turn your weekly sales meetings into *sales practice meetings*.

- Sales meetings are only a waste of time if the team is not using that time to practice and improve on the skills needed to sell.

- A championship team is built by treating the sales team like a professional sports team and weekly sales meetings like a sports team's practice session.

- We have been striving for recognition since we were children and wanted it from our parents and teachers. Now we want recognition from our leaders and peers.

- PRACTICE = KNOWLEDGE = CONFIDENCE = MOTIVATION

11

PRODUCTIVE STREET DAYS

pro•duc•tive (pre 'dek tiv) adj. 1. *Yielding results, benefits, or profit; the power to produce especially in abundance.*

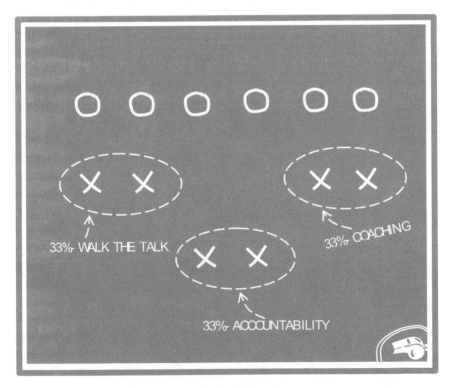

As a leader, it is imperative for you to know what is going on in the field with your team and customers. In the past, many managers found themselves managing from the *ivory tower*. Today, managers are striving to get in the field and take a more 'hands on' approach. Yet, they find themselves more than ever tied to the office in management meetings, dealing with HR issues, and bound to their email and PDA device (oh, yes, at times open access communication can be as big of an inhibitor as it is a contributor). In today's business world, we must manage our time more then ever because our employers and customers are asking us to do more in less time.

One of the main challenges company executives ask me to help them with is motivating and developing their sales teams. There are several approaches I take to aid them in these matters. For some companies, I help kick start them by serving as a keynote speaker at a seminar, sales meeting or training forum. Other companies ask me to come in and provide hands-on coaching. Either way, once my work is complete, the leaders of the company must sustain the effort with their teams to deliver maximum results.

Although this play is the one that leaders often enjoy most, they execute it the least. To help leaders accomplish it on a consistent basis, I am going to give you some ideas to make street days happen.

STREET DAYS: 33% WALK THE TALK

Just as we ask our sales people to prioritize their responsibilities, we as leaders must be willing to do the same. If you were to write down your responsibilities and prioritize them, what would you write?

Mine were the following:

1. Motivate and inspire my team
2. Coach and develop all of my team members and leaders
3. Build, maintain and retain our customer base

4. Handle all executive-level operations

5. Conduct meetings with department heads

Given my first two priorities, it clearly appears that I should be spending about 70% of my time with my team (please note that if 1 and 2 are accomplished, then number 3 will automatically happen). My team, if they are doing their job, should be spending about 90% of their time in the field. Therefore, in order for me to accomplish the goals I have set out, I need to be in the field with them.

By walking the talk, you be able to *show* your sales teams what you expect and how to sell – not just tell them. Your employees will appreciate *the boss* working with them side by side.

However, let me be clear on one thing – there is a difference between going out in the field to monitor (or *police*) your team's performance and working beside them. The type of street day I am talking about here involves you going out side-by-side and doing the work with them in an effort to develop and improve their skills and abilities. In doing so, you send a very positive message, which is: *I will not ask you to do anything that I myself will not do.*

STREET DAYS: 33% - COACHING

In order to accomplish my priorities, I scheduled a minimum of three days per week in the field. An unexpected side benefit from my street days, which were intended to develop my team: every time I was out working with my team, I improved my skills and abilities too.

> "However beautiful the strategy, you should occasionally look at the results."
>
> -- Winston Churchill

Once we were en route to the different field location, I would ask the manager or sales rep what roles they would like me to play at an appointment. This kept them in charge of the meetings and allowed me to see how they wanted to conduct a sales call or negotiate a contract. At the end of the store visits or sales call, we would discuss what each of us thought went well and what we thought we needed to do better next time.

CATCH THE BALL WITH YOUR GLOVE

I remember I was doing a street day with a sales rep whose stores were struggling. As the representative of a product manufacturer, it was the sales rep's job to encourage the retailers to sell our product over the competition's product. After spending ten minutes in the store, I asked one of the store employees to tell me five things about the competition. Without any hesitation, he easily told me five. Then, I asked him to tell me five things about *our* product. With this request, he struggled.

Pulling the sales rep aside, I asked him what he thought of the situation. He casually shrugged and said the store employee just did not get it because he had just trained them last week. In response to his remark, I informed him that it is our fault if our customers do not know our product. It is not up to them to learn by how we teach, but it is up to us to teach by how they learn.

Before leaving the store, we met with the store manager. We discussed the sales reps product knowledge and suggested that if we did a better job training all of the employees on our product, and more importantly how to sell it, that we could help the store increase their overall sales. I recommended that we schedule two training sessions over the next seven days with one additional session every week for the next four weeks. The manager agreed.

Back at the office, I instructed the sales rep's manager to work with him on his training skills. In addition, I asked him to work with all his stores to make sure they truly understood our product and how it benefits them and the customers. With the objectives laid out before them, my manager and his sales rep set to work. By staying disciplined and on task, within 40 days that one specific store increased its sales over 300%!

A larger opportunity came from this experience, which I brought back to my entire team. I realized my team as a whole needed to better understand what the store employees liked and disliked about the competition's products, as well as understand what the customers are looking for when they come into the store.

I also recognized that my team needed to improve their training of the store employees on our product. Specifically, the store employees needed to understand how our products met the needs of their customers. In addition, the store employees needed to understand our commission structure, which was money in their pockets.

The improved store employee training and increased store sales all were brought about by spending one street day in the field.

PUSH ON TOWARDS THE GOAL

To maximize the coaching time with team members in the field, I always rode in their car. I found that made them more comfortable and gave me a chance to spend additional time with them. Sometimes, my reps worked until 9:00 p.m. visiting stores. They would ask me if I needed to be dropped off at the office at 5:00 p.m. My response was always the same, "No, I leave when you leave."

> "Football games are generally won by the boys with the greatest desire."
>
> -- Paul "Bear" Bryant

On average, I spent another four hours during my week, on my own, *inspecting* what I *expected*. I also attended at least two of my managers sales practice meetings with their team. I would try to be as unassuming as possible in an effort to not take over the meeting. Instead, I sat and listened – only contributing when asked.

This showed the team that we were one team with a common goal. In addition, it allowed me the opportunity to conduct on the spot coaching and development.

STREET DAYS: 33% - ACCOUNTABILITY

By this point, you still might be thinking this sounds difficult to do while also focusing on your leadership operational responsibility. Ultimately, it will be you who determines the correct allocation for you and your goals based on your responsibilities and work load. For me, I found I could delegate most of the tasks that did not deal with my top five priorities. Then, I would schedule meetings and other activities around my key priorities.

I lived by a real simple rule, "I have a choice. I could manage my office to mediocrity, or I could coach and develop my team to excellence." For me, it was important that my team found my help and involvement as a supportive tool instead of the boss coming to just "inspect things." I always wanted my involvement to be a good thing – not a bad thing.

I had this one manager who worked for me, but not for long. When I asked him why he did not spend more time with his team in the field, he replied, "I let my people do their jobs and I only get involved when they need me." I told him if you only get involved when there is a problem your involvement symbolizes a bad thing. I later found out that he did not coach them and get involved because he simply was not a good coach. Shortly after that discovery, he found better opportunities outside the company.

YOU CAN OBSERVE A LOT FROM WATCHING

There are two types of street days:

- Scheduled street days
- Unannounced street days

Scheduled street days offer the advantage of allowing the sales reps to schedule meetings with key customers. Field time can be maximized because specific meetings and store visits can be pre-scheduled. It is also a great time for a sales rep to schedule any particularly difficult appointments that they need help on.

Unannounced street days serve a different purpose and can be very interesting. This is a time when you can work with a particular sales rep without them knowing your specific plan. In these instances, I would not call the sales rep until I was close enough to be at any of their locations within 30 minutes. I would call and find out their location and meet them there. If they were doing their job, they would typically respond by saying, "Great, I will see you here." If they happened to not be following a plan or working like they had reported they were, they would be more likely to say, "Uh... how long before you get there... I mean here?" Typically, your performing sales people will enjoy this surprise while the non-performers usually see it as your distrust. I encourage leaders to live by former-President Ronald Reagan's slogan, "Trust, but verify."

DON'T GET ACCUSTOMED TO GOOD LUCK

I once had a manager who I knew was struggling with meeting all of my expectations. So, I took the time to drive two hours out to his territory where he had told me he was planning on working during our morning conversation. At 4:00 p.m., I called to see what location he was at so that I could meet him. He quickly told me that he was actually in another area because of a customer need. Unfortunately for him, we both knew this was a story. So, I asked him to meet me in the office the following morning. When he showed up, we had a talk about what it was going to take to be a leader on a *number one* team. He agreed that what we were doing was the right thing, but recognized that he himself could not do it.

> "When a man has put a limit on what he will do, he has put a limit on what he can do."
>
> -- Charles M. Schwab

As a result, he decided to leave the organization to find a job that better fit his abilities. I respected the manager for recognizing his own dedication and limitations in doing his job. Although I did not like to see people leave the organization, I understood that his decision was the best for the company and our team.

Shortly after his departure, I filled the position with a new manager who was a better fit for the job. This person understood the need to spend time coaching and holding her team accountable. We saw a noticeable difference in the team very quickly and improved sales results soon followed with an increase of 50% in gross sales.

In all aspects of sales leadership, accountability is key to a team's success. Spending time in the field working with your sales reps provides that opportunity to hold your team accountable.

Street days vary from business to business, but for every organization there is a field where the majority of *plays* happen. Some of the most valuable lessons you can learn as a leader take place in the field. Lastly, the majority of leadership responsibilities can be accomplished by spending time on the *streets* including providing guidance, coaching, and *inspecting* what you *expect*.

CHAPTER 11 HIGHLIGHTS

- By walking the talk it allows you to not just tell your sales teams what you expect and how to sell, but gives you, as the leader, the opportunity to show them and coach them.

- Spending time in the field helped my team, and I also learned which made me a better leader and coach.

- I lived by a real simple rule, "I have a choice. I could manage my office to mediocrity or I could coach and develop my team to excellence."

- Spending time in the field working with your sales reps provides that opportunity to hold your team accountable.

- In all aspects of sales leadership accountability is the key to a team's success.

12

TAKING THE BULLET

bul•let ('bŭ let) n. 1. *A round missile to be fired from a firearm; a very fast and accurately thrown ball.*

Taking the bullet – this is a touchy subject for most leaders and organizations. However, the simple truth remains: to be a successful leader you must be willing to do things that most will not. Much like a secret service person's job is to take a bullet for the president, a great leader should always be willing to take a bullet for his team. Sadly, this is a trait that many managers *say* they have. But very few, when put to the test, will actually take a bullet when the time comes.

So, how does a leader 'take the bullet'? For a leader, taking a bullet means to be willing to take the blame, or the fall, for someone who reports to you when they have done something you have directed them to do, or have done something you feel they did with the belief that they were doing the right thing for the company or its customers. Of course, this assumes that their action is legal, ethical, and the overall right thing.

More than ever it seems that leaders are operating from a defensive position. Unfortunately, the acronym CYA (Cover Your *Assets*) is quickly becoming the standard rather than the exception. Take a moment and answer this question, "Are you playing to *not lose* instead of playing to *win*?" If a team only plays defense, the best score they can expect to achieve is *zero* or a *tie*.

ARE YOU REALLY WILLING TO GO OUTSIDE THE BOX?

One of the phrases that companies use today is, "Think outside the box." Another one is, "Go outside the lines." But are you really willing to take the risk or let your team take the risk? Before you answer, "Yes," would you be willing to get fired for it? Today, in corporate America, many managers are so focused on keeping their own jobs they find themselves willing to sacrifice their efforts of truly making a great difference.

Even worse, they are far too willing to sacrifice their own team members to keep from getting fired. I had one simple rule with all of my team members, "I will protect you as long as I am aware of your actions and that you are doing the right thing for the company and the team that is ethical and legal."

Many times during a leader's career, they must make decisions which are right decisions, but do not always line up with a company's policy. A leader must be willing to recognize that sometimes working outside the lines or thinking outside the box will be necessary to do the right thing even if it means getting fired.

> "There is no security in this life, only opportunity."
>
> -- Douglas MacArthur

One leader I had the pleasure to work for was a top performing area vice president. He was one of those leaders that would take a bullet for his team – and we knew it. Many of his peers wondered how he was able to create a team that was so loyal and dedicated to him.

As one of his dedicated followers for years, I can say it was because his team knew that no matter what he was dedicated to them. He told each of us that, if we did something wrong, we were on our own and would suffer the consequences. On the contrary, if we did something that was in the best interest of the company, customer or team (and he was aware of it), then he would take the bullet. Jim walked the talk and his team knew it.

Don't Let the Bad Shots Get to You

Another leader I worked with in the past was the exact opposite. He was a very intelligent person, but did not have loyalty among his team. The ironic thing is because the leader lacked self-awareness he was unaware of the lack of loyalty. The reasoning was simple: the team knew when the going got tough the leader would not be there to help or protect them. Although I enjoyed working with him overall during the few years I reported to him, he did eventually show his true colors during an incident which occurred in 2005.

Based on my proven record at turning around markets, he asked me to help with a market that was under performing and misled for years. He wanted me to go north and implement the same programs I had implemented in the south. Realizing this was a large task involving a lot of change, and like most change, it would not be viewed favorably by all, I still agreed.

I did what he asked, and, in four months, we made more changes for the better than they had over the previous two years. However, a few months into the assignment a human resource issue erupted between one of my peers, who had also been assigned to the project, and a struggling employee.

A human resource committee was assigned to review the matter (which I knew firsthand had been fabricated by the employee in an effort to redirect the issue away from her performance and instead focus on the conduct of her manager). I felt compelled to voice what I knew about the situation and decided to intervene on behalf of my peer. I made a few phone calls to the human resource committee, who had been assigned to review the incident, and told them what I knew.

> "A team will always appreciate a great individual if he's willing to sacrifice for the group."
>
> -- Kareem Abdul-Jabbar

I called my manager immediately after talking to the committee members. In hindsight, I probably should have contacted him first, but I knew without a doubt that it was the right thing to do. At the time, he agreed that the decision by the company was wrong, which brought me great reassurance that I had indeed made the right decision. However, his stance would not last long.

Over the next few months, I found my manager distancing himself from me. To his own admission, he even expressed fear of losing his job regardless of who was right in the matter. In July of 2005, the president of the region came to my office and stated, "You are not going to believe why I am here." After a brief pause, he cleared his throat and calmly announced, "Nathan, you are being fired."

The room fell silent. Once I gained enough composure to speak, I asked him, "Why didn't anybody stand up for me?" He responded, "I was told that anybody who stood in the way would be fired too." In short, I was the person who took the *leader's bullet*. I took the stand to back my peer and was terminated for doing what I knew was ultimately in the best interest of my company, my team and our customers.

There is an interesting end to this story. First of all, it was not more than five months prior to this incident when I had confided in my manager that, upon the completion of the special assignment he had given me, I planned on resigning to start working full-time on my speaking career. So, even though I would never have been able to predict the final method of my departure, it been my plan all along. Although it was a painful way to go, I do not regret the final outcome at all. In fact, I learned two very important lessons from this one incident that I now am able to share with you, which is as follows:

1) Being a great leader means not being afraid to get fired

2) The skills and attributes that makes one successful can also cost one their job

At times, my leadership style was not always liked. However, the majority of individuals who worked for me in the past would agree that my style of leadership was effective. I *was* the type of leader that lived *outside the box* and was always willing to *take the bullet*. The question I ask of you is, "What type of leader are you?"

TRUST YOUR SWING

I have always believed that it is the mission of a leader to make a difference. I contribute my style of leadership and risk-taking to the following attributes:

1) Ignorance of not always knowing when to stop. Finding myself pushing things and people to maximum performance.

2) My confidence (a.k.a. arrogance) which made me believe that I could do anything. It was always my team's job to be number

one, to make the difference, and to do what others would not.

3) My youthful immaturity provided me with few experiences of past failures. Without the limits of failure, my actions and goals were *limitless*.

These attributes led to great success for me and my team. We built four *number one* teams in four different markets. This accomplishment allowed me to become the first and only director in my company's history to achieve this goal. Interestingly enough, at the end of the day, what made me successful also ended up getting me fired.

RUN HARD, THINK BIG!

Since we were small children, we have been told that knowledge is power. However, in business, we have had to re-learn that knowledge is only power when it is combined with action. This concept is imperative to successful leadership.

> Knowledge is only power when it is combined with action.

A person can read all the great leadership books, study leadership classes in college, or take an executive MBA class, but, until a person is able (and willing) to *take action* with the knowledge, they will not have power. In leadership, the *action* can involve many activities such as making tough decisions, motivating team members, developing and teaching team members, or holding the entire team (including oneself) accountable.

Most people *know* what to *do*. However, the successful leaders *do* what they *know*. I wanted to write a book that would not just discuss theory, but give true best practices from sales leaders that I have learned from for more than a decade.

KNOW THE PLAYBOOK

Many times in business we promote sales people to management positions. We give them human resource training, legal training, and business management training.   But rarely do organizations teach managers how to coach.

When I ask people to tell me which person impacted their life the most (outside of parents and family), on average, the people named the most were either sports coaches or teachers.   And the main criterion for selecting these individuals is about the same: the teacher or sports coach expected a lot out of them because they believed in the person's abilities.   A great coach in business is no different.   As leaders and coaches, our people have to know (and believe) that we ask a lot from them and expect great results because we know they are capable of doing it.

Regardless of whether a person has been a manager for one year or twenty years, we can all benefit from coaching.   What I have shared with you are concepts and beliefs I have used, which have been successful for me and others.   This by no means makes them all right (or all wrong).   It just makes them my experience.   If you take two or three ideas from this book to help you improve your leadership skills and abilities, then I have accomplished my goal.

GET OUT OF THE BLOCKS

One of the limitations I have witnessed sales teams place upon themselves is the belief that they already know how to sell because they have been doing it for a long time.   An example of this occurred recently when a speaker's bureau called me to find out if I could do a keynote event for a company's sales force.   Later, they decided to hire a comedian for their sales people because they felt their sales force already knew how to sell.   Always keep in mind that just because your team knows how to sell does not mean they do not need to practice and improve their selling skills.

Always be willing to learn and to practice.

Again, this goes back to sports or any other skill.   Professional football players know how to play football, but if they do not practice they will not get better – and they will stop winning games.   As leaders and managers, it can sometimes be difficult to point at our people as the reason sales are down. It is much easier to blame factors outside of our team's control like the economy, competition, or marketing rather than look inward at our own sales people – or ourselves.

Now, before we explore this concept further, let me make sure I am clear on this point: if a sales team *is responsible* for low sales number, I am not suggesting that the sales team is bad or not doing their job. What I am saying is that, if we do not have a well-designed practice system in place to improve on the basics, then it could easily be that our sales team and we (as their coaches) are to blame.

WHEN THE GUN IS FIRED, YOU'VE GOT TO GO

With an ever-changing competitive landscape and economy, we must continually train our sales people how to sell in and respond to the new conditions and environment. Conducting a one-time training every year is not sufficient. Instead, if you want to make a lasting difference, you must put into place a consistent practice program.

Many times companies might think the solution is to implement a new sales process – and sometimes that is needed. However, more times than not, the team just needs to regularly practice. By practicing, they will improve on the basics of the current system while making adjustments to make it even better.

It is my experience that overall most of the sales methods (although they may have different names or steps that vary from program to program) are fairly similar in structure and process. Regardless of what sales method you follow, the key to building a *number one* sales team is to have a *coach* leading the team who is willing to practice to win.

* * * * *

FINAL THOUGHTS

I hope you have enjoyed this book and that it has brought value to you and your team. As I mentioned in the introduction, I am not a writer by trade. I am a sales person who has successfully led sales teams. I hope you decide to share this book with other leaders and pass it on to new leaders as a way to help them become great coaches.

The topics covered in this book are not rocket science, but they do take time and commitment to implement. When implemented on a consistent basis, they enable any sales team to become a *number one* sales team. I look forward to hearing about your future success!

INDEX

About the Author

For the past decade Nathan Jamail has either been setting sales records, or training others on how to do so. As President of Jamail Development Group, as well as a small business owner himself, Nathan trains, coaches, and mentors sales professionals in many industries. Previously, Nathan set record results in sales by producing top performing sales teams in various capacities including business sales, direct consumer sales, indirect sales, distribution and marketing for several Fortune 100 companies. He has helped develop other executive leaders within Fortune 100 companies, small business owners, and individuals into successful coaches too.

Nathan's passion, energy and leadership have become the center of his success and those around him. He is known as an invincible sales leader with the ability to take the lowest producing areas of the country and build exemplary sales teams. The motto in which he lives by is: "If you BELIEVE, you will ACHIEVE." He implements this principle in businesses and organizations throughout the country. By teaching executive leaders that their number one asset is their employees, companies have seen higher levels of success.

As a practitioner and coach of sales and leadership, Nathan understands that a professional sales person or sales leader cannot be successful with a positive mental attitude alone. He teaches, and more importantly believes, that it takes a great balance of attitude, belief, skill, coaching, and practice to maximize one's skills and attributes for success. Based upon Nathan's first hand experience, clients and organizations are able to identify challenges, maximize employee strengths, and increase productivity. His coaching and training programs have helped organizations increase their productivity up to and over 300%!

Nathan has been featured and interviewed by Fox Television and various other publications regarding his leadership style and the success that he has created. Nathan resides in Frisco, Texas with his wife and two step-children.

NATHAN JAMAIL'S MOST REQUESTED TOPICS

∝ Building and Leading Winning Teams
"How to create and sustain performance"

∝ Influential Selling
"Create referrals by creating relationships"

∝ Team Work of Art Teambuilding and Workshops
"Creatively bringing teams together"

Nathan Jamail, a sought after keynote and motivational speaker is available for your next workshop, meeting, and seminar.

Book him for your next event by contacting your favorite speaker's bureau or log onto www.nathanjamail.com

What people are saying:

"Nathan is a high energy individual and it makes the message more believable when you can see that this guy knows how to be successful. Nathan took a lot of time to learn about our organization and tailor his remarks for our benefit. I would certainly recommend him to any group with new or experienced managers."

Marvin Mutchler
First Savings Bank
President/CEO

"Nathan is one of the strongest sales professionals that I've worked with over the past 12 years. In my opinion, his success is based on his ability to motivate people as well as the ability to teach and train people on the fine art of selling and customer behavior. I highly recommend Nathan Jamail"

> *Charles Moore*
> *Metro PCS*
> *Staff VP, Finance and Operations*

"He is a phenomenal motivational speaker, captivating his audiences and engaging them in discovering and developing their skills and talents, allowing them to accelerate in their personal growth. I would strongly recommend Nathan and encourage anyone who values building and developing their sales teams to benefit from his professional services."

> *Craig Walter*
> *Radio Shack*
> *Senior VP, Consumer Market*

"My agents have expressed how much Nathan's training has helped them to better approach their clients and close more sales. Nathan's training has positively impacted this company. I look forward to your continued support and welcome future trainings. I highly recommend Nathan"

> *Linda Reed*
> *Fenwick Realtors*
> *Vice President*

You can also request information by sending an email to: info@nathanjamail.com.

"I look forward to your future success!" -- *Nathan Jamail*

THE PLAYBOOK ORDER FORM

Give the gift of creating a winning team to all those in your network

◆ Yes, I want _____ copies of The Playbook at $24.95 each (plus $3.49 shipping per book). Please allow 14 business days for delivery. Texas residents please add $2.06 sales tax per book. International orders must be paid by credit card or accompanied by a postal money order in U.S. funds. Please add $7 shipping per book.

◆ My check or money order for $_____ is enclosed.

◆ Please charge my: ◆ Visa ◆ MasterCard

Card #: _____

Expiration Date: _____ Security Code: _____

Signature: _____

Name: _____

Organization: _____

Shipping Address: _____

_____

City/State/Zip: _____

Phone: _____

Email: _____

Billing Address (if different): _____

City/State/Zip: _____

Please make check or money order payable to:
Jamail Development Group
2591 Dallas Parkway Ste 300
Frisco, TX 75034

You can also purchase online at: www.nathanjamail.com